Dance Sense

WITHDRAWN

Dance Sense

Theory and Practice for GCSE Dance Students

Linda Rickett-Young

Northcote House

© Copyright 1997 by Linda Rickett-Young

First published in 1997 by Northcote House Publishers Ltd,
Plymbridge House, Estover Road, Plymouth PL6 7PY, United Kingdom.
Tel: (01752) 202368. Fax: (01752) 202330.
Reprinted 2000.

British Library Cataloguing-in-Data
A catalogue record for this book is available from the British Library.

ISBN 0 7463 0644 X

Typeset by Kestrel Data, Exeter
Printed and bound in Great Britain by The Baskerville Press Ltd, Salisbury.

To my parents

CONTENTS

ILLUSTRATIONS

FOREWORD

A NOTE FOR TEACHERS

This is a text for GCSE Dance students although parts of it may also be found appropriate for use with students both above and below this level. It has been written with the needs of young dancers in mind and I hope it will be used beneficially with them as part of a teaching programme linked to the practical tasks I have included, as well as the examples of choreography, the illustrations and the suggested videos. I hope it will also provide many structured ideas for homework supplemented by teacher-guided reading which places dance in a practical context and encourages an appreciation of other dance works.

While covering all the main elements of the GCSE Dance syllabus it should prove flexible enough to allow a coursework programme to be built around it. It is designed to be used selectively in class rather than worked through slavishly from cover to cover. As dance goes from strength to strength in our schools, I hope young dancers will find it a valuable and enjoyable aid to the development of their skills and appreciation of dance.

FOR THE STUDENT

This book is for you. I hope that first and foremost you enjoy using it and secondly that it helps you to further your understanding of dance. Finally, I hope it helps you to enjoy to the full the fascinating world of dance performance, choreography and appreciation.

ACKNOWLEDGEMENTS

I am greatly indebted to a large number of people who put up with me making a nuisance of myself on repeated occasions. I would like to thank all my friends and colleagues for their repeated enquiries as to the stage the book had reached. This maintained my motivation during its extended creation. In particular Fred Fish Pipes, without whose long-suffering tolerance of my invasion of his office the book would never have been, and also Amanda and Ros.

I would like to acknowledge all the dancers, students and children with whom I have worked over the years. Their enthusiasm and ideas have been a rich source of inspiration to me.

I am most grateful for support from the following: Sarah Woodcock and her staff at the Theatre Museum; Francesca Franchi at the Royal Opera House; Jayne Pritchard, archivist for Rambert Dance Company and English National Ballet; London Contemporary Dance Theatre; Chris Nash; The Laban Centre Library; Erica Stanton and Jane Quinn; Catherine Ashmore.

The author and the publishers gratefully acknowledge the following for supplying illustrations and granting permission for their use.
Catherine Ashmore (plates 1.9, 3.6, 6.3, 8.3); British Museum, London (plates 1.1, 1.2, 1.3); Hugo Glendinning (plate 4.4) with thanks to Erica Bolton and Jane Quinn. James Klosty (plate 3.9); Eleni Leoussi (plate 6.8) with thanks to Arts Administration. Chris Nash (plates 1.8, 3.10, 4.7); Royal Opera House, Covent Garden (plates 1.5, 1.6, 3.1, 4.5); The Collection of the Theatre Museum. By courtesy of the Board of Trustees of the Victoria and Albert Museum (plates 1.4, 1.7, 2.1, 2.3, 2.5, 3.2, 3.3, 3.4, 4.1, 4.6, 6.2); photographers: Anthony Crickmay (plates 2.5, 3.2, 3.3, 3.4, 4.6); Fred Pipes (plates 4.2, 6.5).

ONE ■ A HISTORY OF DANCE

Throughout this book there are photographs and examples of dance from history to the present day. This chapter does not cover the history of all dance forms in society: to do so would need a separate book.

What follows gives some idea of how we arrived at where we are now. What events in the past led to you reading this book? Where did the dance that we see at the theatre today originate? What are its influences from the past?

THE EVOLUTION OF DANCE

Dance in Early Times

Dance is found among all peoples of the world, indeed, some say that it is the oldest art form. Today, as in earlier communities, dance is still an important part of social and religious life, and is performed by everyone. Such communities are usually ones which still depend on hunting and agriculture for their living and they may even support a dancer as a professional within the village. All social occasions such as birth, death, harvest, coming-of-age, and healing are marked by dancing in order to communicate with the unseen gods and goddesses. In this way the wellbeing of the community is blessed and assured.

Whether in Africa, Asia, Europe, America or the Pacific symbolic movement is used where speech alone may not be enough. The intricate hand gestures or *mudras* of Indian dance are an example of this or, on a simpler level, the dance of eastern Europe which features high jumps, supposedly to encourage crops to grow. The power of movement can say more than many words. The sun, moon, stars, seasons, animals, all influence the rituals and dances of these communities and create powerful beliefs and incredible physical feats. A *Sufi* dervish spinning for twelve or fifteen hours without dizziness, an Indonesian trance dancer thrusting knives onto bare chests so strongly that the blades bend are just two examples.

In Britain today we see many examples of dance from other cultures such as Indian, African, and flamenco which have grown and evolved. Dance by Shobana Jeyasingh and other classical Indian dancers reveals how an ancient style has developed within a foreign culture. Her dance deals with sophisticated concepts of time and space and often uses modern western music like that of Michael Nyman. Similarly such pan-African groups as Adzido present works such as *Coming Home*, and in accompanying workshops attempt to make the dance and music accessible to all sections of the community. In a rich multi-cultural Britain there is a real melting-pot of dance.

In Europe ancient ceremonies are still to be found even though the original pagan dances have long since been christianised or have disappeared altogether. In Barcelona you can still see the Catalonians perform their national circle dance, the *Sardana*. This is a symbol of their identity and was banned on threat of imprisonment under the government of General Franco, such was its power! In eastern Europe too, where an agricultural lifestyle is still dominant, there are many customs such as carnival processions with animals and decorative costume to celebrate the arrival of spring. In Bulgaria one dance features women dancing around a barrel, jumping as high as possible to make the crops grow. In Britain the Morris dance is the ghost of early fertility rites. The Scottish Highland Sword dance or *Fling* would have originally been to celebrate victory in battle, perhaps danced on the shield of an opponent.

The prehistoric cave paintings in France are tens of thousands of years old and depict war dances and healing dances. Our first real knowledge of dance comes from the early civilizations of Sumeria, Assyria, Egypt and Greece. These people left written records and art objects which show clearly processions and ritual dances to their deities. Dancers were trained in order to perform in the many acts of worship, like the dance of stars which was based on the movements of the solar system and supposedly influenced rain, crops and survival. Gradually dancing became a profession for entertaining the upper classes. Similar processes happened in ancient Greece, but here dance was also part of education. Plato wrote 'to sing and dance well is to be well educated.'

In ancient Rome life was lived to the full and rituals became excessive. Dance did not escape abuse, and it was therefore hardly surprising that the early christians associated dance with their persecution and suffering. Throughout the Dark and Middle Ages dance was disapproved of and

1.1   Relief of Dancing Girls in Thebes c. 1500–1400 BC

1.2   Terracotta relief 1st century AD. *A maenad and a satyr dance with the infant Dionysos*

3

discouraged. As Christianity spread through Europe dance was only allowed if it was based on a holy theme. This resulted in dance being performed in the churches. Often pagan festivals were still celebrated, masked as Christian holy days with churches built on top of existing pagan shrines.

Such unusual dances as *The Dance of Death* and weird *Danseomania* spread during the fourteenth century through to the fifteenth century, still showing their pagan roots. So the peasants continued to dance in circles, chains and couples to be copied and refined by the nobility. Even today in Spain, *Bal de la Mort* is still danced during Holy Week. Twelve men and three women dress in black on which skeletons are painted and they process the town to the sound of a single drum.

The Birth of Ballet

In castles and palaces across Europe the nobility feasted and dance flourished. The first dancing masters appeared in Italy in the 1400s. The Italian word *ballere* means 'to dance' and is the word from which ballet is derived. Extravagant spectacles were held akin to our modern day nightclub cabaret, telling myths and legends and stories of important events. Dancing masters appeared and set standards of etiquette. All the gentlemen were expected to be accomplished dancers.

By the end of the 1500s dancing was high fashion at the courts of Europe and so ballet was born. At this time, the typical upright carriage of the body, turn-out, the five positions and the basic steps were developed by the Italian and French aristocracy. By the 1600s ballet was performed in actual theatres, allowing the audience to see it from the front. This separation of performer and viewer led to the professional form of ballet as we now know it.

The opening of the Paris Opera Ballet School in 1713 guaranteed the development of choreographer, principal dancer and *corps de ballet*. The coming of the Romantic era from about 1830 gave rise to such famous works as *La Sylphide* (1832) by Filippo Taglioni for his daughter Marie Taglioni and August Bournonville's version in 1836 for the Royal Danish Ballet which still survives today. The training of dancers was also evolving and the nineteenth century innovation of dancing *en pointe* emphasised the romantic 'heavenly' nature of ballet as seen in the famous painting by Degas.

1.3 *Court and rustic dance. 16th century engraving by Theodor de Bry*

MADEMOISELLE TAGLIONI.

1.4 *Marie Taglioni*

Eventually a combination of the Franco Prussian war and excessive decadence led the ballet into decline. Standards of choreography and technique declined. This was to be the end of Paris as the leader in the world of ballet.

Russia to the Rescue

Russia always copied European trends and fashions and ballet was no exception. In 1766 it received royal patronage and in 1847 French born Marius Petipa moved to St Petersburg and stayed there for almost 60 years. Ballet thrived in Russia, and was still quite respectable at a time when in Europe it was considered morally questionable. Petipa was producing choreography of large ballets with great variety in styles tinged with a new sort of toughness. His production of the *Sleeping Beauty*, was outstanding in its beauty and demanded all the skills of the excellent dancers from the Imperial School.

By the early twentieth century Russian ballet was technically the best but its creativity declined until Mikhail Fokine began to work in St Petersburg. He questioned the old ways and formulas and introduced new ideas. He moved in artistic circles which brought him in contact with entrepreneur Serge Diaghilef who was to become director of the new ballet company of which Fokine would be the principal choreographer.

1.5 The six fairies from the Diaghilef Ballet production of THE SLEEPING PRINCESS *(1921)*

Task 1

Watch a video of *Les Sylphides* (1908), choreography Mikhail Fokine for Imperial Ballet Theatre, Russia, music by Chopin. Notice and explain the following:
1. How do the movements of the dance give it a romantic look?
2. What kind of group shapes and patterns do the *corps de ballet* use?
3. In what ways does this dance differ from the earlier traditional ballet of Imperial Russia?

The New Approach

Diaghilef decided to export Russian ballet to the rest of Europe. He showed off Fokine's *Firebird* set to Stravinsky's music and *Schéhérazade* (music, Rimsky-Korsakof) with Leon Bakst's sumptuous set and costumes. The Paris audience was won over, seeing a refreshing mix of expression of complex feelings, strong male dancing and unity of style, music and visual setting. So Diaghilef's 'Ballets Russes' was taken out of Russia and performed by many famous dancers such as Pavlova and Karsavina. Famous composers like Prokofiev and Debussy, artists like Bakst and Benois and choreography not only from Fokine but Vaslav Nijinsky, Leonide Massine, Bronislava Nijinska and George Balanchine all collaborated in this ballet revival.

Fokine was considered to be the father of modern ballet. In his footsteps came Vaslav Nijinsky – dancer extraordinary with his soaring jumps who was also encouraged by Diaghilef to choreograph. His *L'Après Midi d'un Faune* outraged Parisian audiences in its overt symbolism, regarded by its audience as obscene. His *Le Sacré du Printemps* (Stravinsky) caused a riot because of its unconventional score depicting a pagan ritual, with its use of uneven rhythmic pounding and off-beat accents.

The company continued to work until Diaghilef's death in 1929. His dancers and choreographers left to carry the legacy to new parts of the world. Artists such as George Balanchine travelled as far away as the USA.

In Britain Marie Rambert and Ninette de Valois built on Diaghilef's policy and started to build a British 'ballet club'. Names such as Alicia Markova, Margot Fonteyn, Antony Tudor and Frederick Ashton formed

1.6 Nijinsky in SCHÉHÉRAZADE *(1910)*

the beginnings of the Ballet Rambert (1935) and the Royal Ballet (originally Vic-Wells Ballet 1931), now two of Britain's leading companies. In 1966 the now renamed Rambert Dance Company became more of a modern dance company, featuring works in the Graham style by Norman Morrice and Glen Tetley. Later, under directors John Chesworth, Christopher Bruce and Robert North this tendency became more pronounced. Later still, under the direction of Richard Alston, the Cunningham influence dominated.

Similarly, in 1926 Dame Ninette de Valois, with help from theatre owner Lilian Bayliss, brought ballet back to the Sadler's Wells Theatre. The first performance starred Alicia Markova and Anton Dolin to be followed later by Margot Fonteyn and Robert Helpmann. In 1935, after having worked with Rambert, Frederick Ashton joined as choreographer. In 1956 Sadler's Wells received a Royal Charter and became known as the 'Royal Ballet'. It started a touring section in addition to the main body. In 1963 Ashton became director, passing to Kenneth Macmillan in 1970. Throughout the focus was on English choreography and the classics. Typical of these works were Ashton's light-hearted and witty *Façade* (1931) to music by William Walton and the simple rural frolics of *La Fille Mal Gardée* (1960). He also revived Nijinsky's *Les Noces* and made work for the partnership of Fonteyn and Rudolf Nureyev. Under Macmillan the focus was the same but with more emphasis on full length dance-dramas like *Mayerling* (1978) and more modern classical work like Tetley's plotless *Gemini* (1977). Under Norman Morrice's directorship, Sadler's Wells Royal Ballet emphasised the modern style. Then in 1986 ex-dancer Anthony Dowell took over and continued to use fewer guest choreographers and to encourage in-house work. He also invited Alston to choreograph *Midsummer* in 1983. Now home-grown choreographers such as Ashley Page and David Bintley feature regularly alongside a staple of well-loved classics and full-length works like Macmillan's *The Prince of the Pagodas* (1989) to music by Benjamin Britten.

Recently part of the company moved to new premises and is now known as the Birmingham Royal Ballet. The Diaghilef legacy was thus developed in Great Britain to become a distinctive British style of ballet performed by a strong modern company with a tradition of nurturing young choreographers, musicians and artists.

1.7 LES RENDEZVOUS (1933) choreography Frederick Ashton

THE MODERN DANCE ERA

As Diaghilef and his associates were revolutionising the ballet other rebels were appearing with ideas and approaches that had little to do with that world. In the United States of America the accepted form of ballet was being rejected by the dancers themselves who wanted to find their own ways of moving.

Loie Fuller was known for her dances using skirts and scarves in coloured light. As the electric light was the discovery of the time this gave her show exotic glitter and interest. She was shadowed eventually by the untrained genius of Isadora Duncan who, as an outspoken feminist, believed in a woman's right to love and bear her children as she pleased. This would have been a scandalous opinion at the time. She dared to dance in the face of America's puritan heritage and she shocked everyone with her use of flimsy, loose clothes, bare feet, simple improvisation, bare stage and her ambitious use of classical 'greats' such as the music of Beethoven and Wagner. Her lone, liberal free-spirit won acclaim in Europe and America, and set a path for others to follow.

At the same time Ruth St Denis trod the boards with spontaneity and individuality. For her, a cigarette advertisement showing an Egyptian goddess inspired her own style of dance which was exotic and mysterious. She met Ted Shawn in 1914 who was first her pupil and later husband. Together they formed the company Denishawn and offered classes in Spanish, Oriental, American-Indian dance and ballet. One of their students, was Martha Graham. The company toured and later Shawn formed the first all-male ballet company, setting a path for others to follow. St Denis was to influence many dance-artists such as Fokine, Marie Rambert, Martha Graham and others as an inspirational and innovatory free spirit.

By the time of the Great Depression the exotic gave way to a hardening of feeling. Martha Graham was very serious in making hard-edged dance technique and choreography as described in later chapters. Its importance lies in its point of view, that is, that the individual choreographer is a priority. It is not merely a technique or a date that makes 'modern dance'. Graham rebelled against Denishawn just as Duncan had against ballet. So in the early 1920s and 30s dance began to metamorphose into a new look.

In America and Germany where ballet had little prestige, modern dancers experimented relentlessly. The resultant look was often hard, stark and earthy, and usually the work of women as society reeled from the perfume of the romantic ballet which labelled male dancing as effeminate. Women like Martha Graham, Doris Humphrey, Hanya Holm and Mary Wigman announced their independence from traditional thought, preferring to be known as women and artists through their work. Interestingly, men of the time who were associated with dance were often initially associated with music or acting and found their way to dance via these other forms. Such men were Emile Jacques-Dalcroze and Rudolf Laban whose analytical theories informed the work of Wigman and Holm. As a result of the Second World War dance in Germany faded but the ideas were passed on to the United States by Hanya Holm who stayed there and continued to develop the principles along lines which suited the American temperament, physique and culture.

Meanwhile in Britain important advances were being made in dance education as Rudolf Laban, exiled by the war, introduced his theories into the world of modern educational dance. Perhaps you are reading this book as part of your studies for a GCSE or A Level in dance. If so you are a part of the legacy of Laban. He was the leader of the Central European school of modern dance and his work embraced many areas from his well-known system of dance notation *Labanotation*, to his movement choirs *Bewegungschore*, the pure expression of human involvement in the dance of the cosmos. His pupils and collaborators were many and included Kurt Jooss and Lisa Ullmann. He also worked on analysing movement in industrial processes. By the 1950s modern dance was established – seemingly a North American phenomenon, but there was more to follow. The early pioneers gave rise to another generation of choreographers; Paul Taylor, Eric Hawkins and Alwin Nikolais to name just a few, who each had their own distinctive styles. Not least was a pupil of Martha Graham called Merce Cunningham who maintained the tradition of the new by producing controversial and challenging dance that announced yet another revolution to challenge dance audiences.

Merce Cunningham was a dancer with Graham but he developed his ideas which conflicted with hers. Insisting that dance is only about dancing and developing a new technique to express his idea he took dance into the next era. 'I don't even want a dancer to start thinking that a movement means something. That was what I really didn't like about working with Martha Graham; the idea that was always being given to you that a particular movement meant something specific. I thought that was nonsense.'[1]

His technique combined almost balletic footwork with rapid shifts of weight and direction, a mobile spine and cascading rhythms. As well as this, his use of chance methods to construct dances, his attitude to the stage space being an open, many-sided area and his idea that movement, music and set are independent of each other (often only coming together for the first time in performance) reflect his associations with other art forms. Composer John Cage and artists like Andy Warhol and Robert Rauschenberg would be his fellow conspirators in the forming of radical ideas that, even though first rejected, are now a part of the mainstream of dance. Cunningham's dances are now in the repertoires of Rambert Dance Company and New York City Ballet.

Martha Graham, too, was to have a worldwide significance, and here in Britain in the 1960s hotelier Robin Howard was so impressed by her work that he set up a trust to allow her technique to be taught in London.

The chosen director was ex-Graham dancer Robert Cohan and so in 1967 the London Contemporary Dance Theatre was formed. It has given birth to several of Britain's leading choreographers including Siobahn Davies, Richard Alston, Robert North and Tom Jobe. Through touring, workshops and residencies a massive new audience was created for contemporary dance in Britain. For a long time Cohan's style, softer than that of Graham, but still full of movement with meaning, was most obvious in the company's performances. Examples are the humorous *Waterless Method of Swimming Instruction* (1974), the haunting *Cell* (1969) and the lyrical, biblical *Stabat Mater* (1975). When Cohan retired in 1989 Dan Waggoner took over as director. His training with both Graham and Cunningham offered an interesting if subtle change of look for LCDT. In 1991 the American Nancy Duncan became artistic director. She likes to present many different types of work from choreographers such as Jayne Dudley with her classic Graham solo *Harmonica Breakdown* (1938) to the radical work of Arnie Zane *Freedom of Information* and in-house dance such as by Jonathon Lunn. It seems fitting after nearly a century that the company founded on the pioneer work of a woman should be directed by one. Indeed there is

---

[1]Merce Cunningham, *Saturday Review Press* (1975), ed. James Klosky, Dutton.

1.8 *FREEDOM OF INFORMATION choreography Arnie Zane*

much room for speculation about the role of women in the world of dance as we move into the twenty-first century. At the beginning of the twentieth century many powerful women led the dance world into a new era. Gradually the power seems to have passed to the hands of men. Possibly there were not enough women to hand the work on to. Perhaps the way forward will begin to reintroduce women as choreographers and directors rather than as in the role of dancer only. Certainly the question of sexual politics and stereotypes was to be an important part of dance as it grew into the 1960s.

Task 2

Watch excerpts from the following videos;
Robert North, *Death and the Maiden*;
Richard Alston, *Soda Lake*;
Christopher Bruce, *Sergeant Early's Dream*.
Answer the following questions:
1. Which of the three is concerned more with Graham's idea of movement that has meaning and which is concerned with movement for its own sake?
2. Which shows a Graham style of movement and which does not? Describe the style of one which is *not* in a Graham style.
3. What is the content of each?
4. How does each of them use accompaniment and how does it help to make the expression clearer?

AFTER THE MODERN

The post modern dance genre began its rich era of experiment when in New York in the 1960s even Cunningham was thought of as too restricted. As ever, dance responded to more general trends in society. The decade represented challenge to any and all authority: young people questioned civil rights, the Vietnam war, sexual liberation, the law and demanded to be 'free'. Young dancers questioned the need for technique, seeing it as being too rigid and they asked the ultimate question 'what *is* dance?' This gave rise to exploration in every direction.

In 1962 the co-operative group the Judson Dance Theatre began. Most of them were from the Cunningham studio and company, and they rebelled against the existing *avant-garde* to form another one! Names like Trisha Brown, Yvonne Rainer, Steve Paxton, David Gordon decided that technique was too limiting, abandoned the trained bodies of dancers, made all decisions which affected the group collectively and rejected the proscenium stage and repertory. They were interested in everyday movement rather than that which was theatricalised and therefore – in their eyes – artificial, and they used non-dancers in their work. Dance appeared on rooftops, in parks, streets and museums. Others were to bring modern dance and ballet closer and rejected the sexual stigmas attached to dance which they regarded as being limiting

1.9 OPAL LOOP *(1989)* *choreography Trisha Brown*

and unjust. Dancers appeared naked to make the point that gender and nudity were not important.

The world of painting was exploring similar issues, for example using pedestrian objects like the soup cans of Andy Warhol. The 'Happenings' of the sixties emphasised spontaneity, natural movement, audience participation, basically anything 'far-out' and the further out the better! This, of course, can only echo the radical work of Isadora Duncan and her belief in the truth of only what is natural. In some ways a circle was being completed.

Prior to this the only traditions which had maintained touch with improvisations were those in the Central European style, the tradition of Hanya Holm and her students. However, in Europe itself one individual, Pina Bausch, trod new ground in the steps of the Central European style. A direct descendant of the Laban-Jooss school, she replaced deeper emotions into movement and performance. Her work reveals the stark reality of twentieth century life, its isolation, violence, humour, horror and psychoanalysis. Her influence spread all over Europe.

In Britain the flagship of the post modern movement is New Dance. Such companies as DV8 led by Lloyd Newson reveal interest in issues of sexual politics as well as the darkness of the Bausch/European style. Other exponents of New Dance show a typical wide variety of approaches. The minimal repetition and calm contemplation of Rosemary Butcher's work contrasts with that of the Cholmondeleys which is full of wry humour, feminist strategy and rich in unusual gesture. Ian Spink's work with Second Stride blends dance, music, design and dialogue in an almost opera-like way.

Similarly dance by Motionhouse and Laurie Booth builds on Steve Paxton's approach and his style of contact improvisation. There is also concern that dance should be for everyone whatever age, race or disability. Both Laurie Booth and Motionhouse have worked with groups of special needs people and also combined them with professional dancers in performance.

Task 3

Watch the following videos by Motionhouse: *The House of Bones* and *Different Dancers Similar Motion.* As you watch note down answers to the following questions:
1. How is the movement style characteristic of New Dance?
2. When and where was this style first discovered and by whom?
3. Why is working with groups who have special needs typical of New Dance?
4. What is the main concern of *The House of Bones*?
5. What do you think is the main concern of New Dance?

Task 4

Research an issue of concern like homelessness, child abuse, caring for the environment and discuss it in a group. From improvisation make a short group dance. Find suitable accompaniment and a title.

Various companies have done and still do work under this umbrella and indeed a whole annual event called *Dance Umbrella* promotes new dance every November. Even though it is centred in London it stages events all over the UK and as well as performance it includes video, film, open discussions, leaving room for the ongoing exchange of opinion which is the very lifeblood of such a style. Similarly in France, Belgium and Holland names like Maguy Marin, Anne Teresa De Keersmaeker and Daniel Larrieu present more diverse individual work.

Chapter 9 covers dance in the 1990s in more detail.

Further Reading

The History of Dance, Mary Clarke and Clement Crisp, Orbis.

The Dance Handbook, Allen, Robertson and Hutera, Longman.

The Magic of Dance, Margot Fonteyn, BBC Publications.

The Encyclopedia of Dance and Ballet, Mary Clarke and David Vaughan, Peerage Books.

Ballet: An Illustrated History, Clarke and Crisp, A & C Black.

Dance, Jack Anderson, Newsweek Books.

Terpsichore in Sneakers, Sally Banes and Robert Alexander, Houghton Mifflin Co.

Dance from Magic to Art, Lois Ellfeldt, WCB.

May I have the Pleasure? The story of popular dancing, Belinda Quirey, BBC.

Modern Ballet, John Percival, Herbert.

Videos

Indian Dance, ILEA Learning Resources Branch, TV and Publishing Centre, Thackeray Rd, London SW8 3TB.

Adzido Dance Co. 'Coming Home', National Resource Centre for Dance, University of Surrey, Guildford.

Les Sylphides, an Evening with the Royal Ballet.

Bolshoi Ballet live-divertissements.

American Ballet Theatre at the Met.

'Paris Dances Diaghilef', Paris Opera Ballet.

Motionhouse, *The House of Bones* and *Different Dancers Similar Motion* available from Oxford Independent Video, Pegasus Theatre, Magdalen Rd, Oxford OX4 1RE. Tel 01865-250150.

TWO ■ THE SKILL OF DANCE

A STARTING POINT – DANCE TECHNIQUE

As your body matures it will require new challenges in dance. Technical training is demanding, especially at first, but it is also fun. In a dance class the harder you work, the more you will build up skills and confidence.

There are many styles of dance technique; ballet, contemporary and jazz are perhaps the most familiar, but they all have a common aim, that is to:

- make the body more mobile;

- strengthen the body;

- develop awareness of the body centre;

- develop co-ordination;

- widen your awareness of movement possibilities;

- help to develop confidence in your own body.

The dancer's body is an instrument. Like a piano, it must be tuned, but this is only the start. Technique alone is not enough, it needs to be combined with imagination in order to create dances. This cocktail of technique and imagination will stimulate new ideas for moving which are appropriate to whatever you may wish to express. Eventually you will be able to compose dances which reveal your own special style.

Some dancers who have created their own styles of technique and choreography are shown on the following pages. These styles are physically demanding and in schools a 'softer' technique is more appropriate. This is reflected in dance exercises. Exercises are designed to assist the young dancer to move correctly, confidently and with a sense of enjoyment.

2.1 Martha Graham in Imperial Gesture

THE CLASS

'The mind is a muscle'
Yvonne Rainer[1]

On a simple physical level the class starts usually with a series of safe warm-up exercises to release tensions and prepare the muscles and the mind.

Vulnerable areas of the body such as the back, shoulders, neck, hips,

[1]Yvonne Rainer, *The Vision of Modern Dance* (1980), ed. Jean Morrison Brown, Dance Books, p141. This was the title of a dance and an account of her work, written in 1965 and published in 1975.

2.2 *Graham's unique use of the spine in contractions and release is still influential in dancers who train at The Place, London. London Contemporary Dance Theatre in Residency at I. M. Marsh College, Liverpool 1974*

knees, ankles and feet should be carefully warmed, relaxed and extended. You should try to feel that you are 'getting into' your body, like trying on some new clothes. There should also be some thought given to how the skeleton and muscles work and how breathing affects the flow of energy.

EXERCISE 1: a combination exercise to use for warming up.
Start with the feet shoulder width apart, arms raised above the head.

a. Step in place 4 times and each time stretch up through the ribs and on throughout the fingertips.

b. **CHECK** that as you step you go through the whole foot smoothly – toe, ball, heel – and that your arms stay above your head. **STRETCH AS FAR AS YOU CAN.**

c. Bring the feet closer (under the hip bones) drop the arms and feel the abdominal muscles pull up. Breathing in, roll down, head leading to *d*; bend your knees as you do this. You should feel a comfortable stretch in your back. Breathe out and stretch the legs dropping the head and keeping your weight forwards. Feel a stretch through the hamstrings *e*. Do not worry if you cannot keep your hands on the floor, try to stretch without too much strain. Now roll up with bent knees that gradually straighten. When standing start again. Repeat 4 times.

This exercise stretches the feet, legs, back and it strengthens the abdominal muscles. Try to breathe deeply all the time and allow the stretch to deepen into the joints.

EXERCISE 2: to strengthen the abdominals and the back while also stretching the backs of the legs.

a. Lie on the floor, back flat and weight on the feet.

b. Breathe in through the nose and trail the arms on the floor, gradually raising them above the head. Breathe out through the mouth and push down to contract the abdominal muscles. This will make the upper torso curve up and raise the arms in front of you.

c. Hold briefly, keeping the head back. You may feel a stretch in your back. Now keep pushing down and let the hands lift you up to sitting *d.* Feel light, 'floaty' and tall.

Allowing your natural body weight to drop over in a curve *e.*, swing down over straight legs *f.* Rebound from bent elbows, and as the arms shoot forward again rise to *g.* – stretch legs and feet and feel tall!

Finally open chest to the ceiling, drop the head back and arch backward. Fingertips support you to lie down *h.* Bend legs in and start again. Repeat 4 times.

EXERCISE 3: a good swing exercise to mobilise your waist.

a. Stand in parallel (feet under hips), arms to side.

b. Swing your arms side to side wrapping them around the body and opening them each time.

You can also do this stepping with the direction of the swing and you can allow the momentum of the swing to take you into a 3 step turn sideways. It is fun to experiment with what else the swing can take you into.

a)   b)

Exercises such as slow shoulder rotations, overhead arm stretches, rolling down and up, from standing, and careful trudging on the spot are a few useful ones.

More demanding stretches and exercises should now be introduced for strengthening of the abdominal muscles, the backs and the legs, as well as more energetic swings and more demanding extensions.

Task 1

- After a class make a list of as many exercises as you can remember. Describe what each one is for. Use counts and diagrams if it is helpful.

Discuss.

- How do you feel at the end of a technique class?
- What has happened to you?

CENTERING

'That little magnet in the centre that holds you together'
Hanya Holm[1]

After a number of technique classes you may detect a difference in the way you feel. One of the most obvious ways in which you may notice a change is in your posture. Good posture is vital for control, safety and expression. We say that the body is correctly **aligned**, ie it forms a straight line from head to feet. There should be a feeling of freedom, easy movement, effortless carriage of the head and an awareness of energy travelling out in all directions from the centre to all body parts. In this way you can 'move away' from your centre of balance while still retaining your poise.

One of the causes of poor alignment is the blocking effect of tension, eg lifted or rounded shoulders or sticking the hips out backwards. The exercises at the start of class should help you to learn how to relax muscles when they are not needed. Correct use of the various muscle groups is the only way to bring the skeleton into alignment. In this way you will become more balanced and be able to move efficiently and expressively.

Task 2

Carry this out in pairs, one checking, one moving. Stand still. Check:

- Feet parallel – line them up under the hips. Check that the insides of the heel and big toe are in a straight line.
- Lift the arches of the feet so that the weight of the body is distributed under the heel, big toe and outside front edge of the foot, and evenly on both feet.
- Thighs slightly lifted to support hips.
- Energise and lift abdominal muscles, drop tail bone. Feel the back wide and supporting the arms.
- Lengthen the neck, let the head float, drop the shoulders.
- Tighten buttocks.

[1]Hanya Holm, *Vision of Modern Dance*, p74.

- Breathe in 'through the soles of the feet' and let the breath flow up through the body opening, filling and softening all the joints.
- Breathe out through the top of the head.

Do Not:

- —Lift shoulders
- —Hold breath
- —Drop/lift chin
- —Tuck hips under
- —Tilt them forwards.

- **Now** feel this position and rise easily onto a half-toe. Swing arms easily and move head without loss of balance. Use your bones for support and feel control from your centre outwards into space.

You may try this either with legs parallel or turned out. Both positions require you to connect heels to the tops of your legs so that control of the legs always uses the large upper leg muscles, rather than the more vulnerable knees and ankles.

Good alignment is not still; it is a dynamic readiness for movement. Watch when someone starts to walk – the body tilts forward. As they walk the 'plumb line' remains. Energy is wasted if sections of the body need to be corrected and pulled into line. In order to balance, the muscle groups must be stretched and strengthened to increase:

1. **Flexibility**: the range of movement in the joints which is increased by lengthening the muscle fibres; and
2. **Strength**: the amount of work muscle can do before fatigue sets in which is developed by increasing repetitions of movement or the use of weight on a muscle during exercise.

Once you begin to feel a sense of central control, moving and co-ordination will be easier. Trained dancers appear to move easily, confidently and expressively on stage because they have built an instinctive sense of alignment from their centre. Centering is both physical and psychological. It refers to *a*) the centre of weight of a body and *b*) feeling whole and grounded **IN** the body.

The centre of gravity is the most dense portion in the body, in the pelvis slightly below the navel. Being 'centred' operates as a feeling of correctness and ease, a oneness with motion. When moving correctly it increases the dancer's ability to express the sense of the dance through the accuracy of movement and the projection of the meaning to the audience.

ACTION TIME!

'Your training gives you freedom'
Martha Graham[1]

So now you have an awareness of your centre – but can you move and yet remain aligned? The joints of your body are capable of only three simple movements:

- FLEXION (bending)
- EXTENSION (stretching)
- ROTATION (turning).

We will use the torso to illustrate these simple movements.

The torso can bend in any direction with a round or straight spine:

and it can do this in sections too, ie only the upper torso:

[1]Martha Graham, *Prime Movers* (1977), Joseph H. Mazo, A & C Black Ltd, p157.

It can also extend:

Its individual sections rotate separately: head, ribs and hips. Indeed, such hip rotations are quite a noticeable feature in jazz dance techniques such as that of the American Matt Mattox.

It is interesting to note that the skeleton and muscles of the body function as a simple machine. For example whenever a part of the body bends (flexes), the corresponding side of that part will stretch. So if you bend your arm the biceps flexes while the triceps stretches. The richness of dance arises from the many combinations of these simple functions. In the *Martha Graham Technique*, when a contraction appears the abdominals flex and the back muscles stretch, giving the torso a characteristic appearance. Similarly in the *Cunningham Technique* there is an interest in the upper, middle and lower sections of the spine curving independently as well as together. This gives the spine a more vertical stance akin to that of classical ballet, but with more possibilities of mobility. In both styles the spine functions as a separate limb.

More recently, *Release Techniques* of New Dance focus on how the body moves anatomically in a series of small, slow, gentle movements. The aim is to awaken understanding of how muscles, joints and organs actually work. Such systems as the *Alexander Technique* and *Feldenkrais* fall into this category. Both of these approaches concentrate on how movement *feels* rather than its outward appearance. The following exercise is an example:

Standing easily, concentrate on breathing, imagining it filling and emptying the body. See it as light which brightens the rooms of your body and see the ribs and diaphragm muscle increasing the space for air as you inhale. As you exhale the space decreases. Take 10 minutes or so to do this and so feel how breath works and how it can help movement to be both safer and more adventurous. It may even encourage you to yawn! Sounds wonderful!

Task 3

In pairs, try the three basic actions while sitting, kneeling, standing and lying down, using fingers, toes, ankles, shoulders, elbows, hips etc. Always try to connect the body parts to your centre and isolate the part so that it is the only part moving. Make a simple phrase which you can dance, mirroring your partner.

These isolated gestures can feel and look quirky, but when they are combined endless numbers of complicated actions result.

THE FIVE PRINCIPAL DANCE ACTIONS

After warming up the class concentrates on more complex combinations of movements, which are combinations of the five following actions:

1. TRAVELLING
2. JUMPING
3. TURNING
4. GESTURE
5. STILLNESS.

1. Travelling

This consists of basic stepping patterns; rolling, sliding and crawling. Singly or in combination they can make interesting rhythms and spatial patterns. Some basic step patterns are listed below.

- **Walk** – even rhythm. In a natural walk the heel goes to the floor first. Sometimes a walk is stylised so that the toes touch first. Pull up the centre to keep smooth control and alignment.
- **Run** – a fast walk needing more foot and leg extension.
- **Prance** – a run with a lift of the knees. Requires strong foot extension so that the free knee lifts up sharply.
- **Triplet** – a stylised walk in a 3/4 rhythm. Smooth, waltz-like. Merce Cunningham once remarked that when humans invented the waltz they must have felt like they needed three feet. Why do you think this is?

Other patterns include:

Skip (hop, step)
Slide (glide step, cut step)
Gallop (step, cut step)
Polka (hop step, step, draw step)
Schottische (step, draw step, step, hop)
Mazurka (glide step, cut step, hop).

All of the above usually hold the arms or let them swing freely in opposition to the legs for balance. However, once you feel comfortable with them you can use your imagination and experiment with different uses of the arms. You can also alter the speed, direction, dynamics and floor pattern.

Task 4

1. Try triplets very slowly and gradually accelerate until they become running.
2. Change a walk from being light and continuous to strong and interrupted.

What might these changes express to an onlooker?

Stepping patterns form a rich range of movement for folk and social dances. At the time of Elizabeth I the peasants were known as the 'Dancing English'. Until the 19th century life styles were mainly isolated and agricultural-based, but when the cotton and wool industries grew up many people moved into the towns and much of the traditional music and dance was lost. Interestingly, dance lost its masculine status, and today only the shadows of this remain in *morris dance*. Originally men were trained to dance at the solstices to awaken the earth or scare away evil. These pagan rituals were less significant in town life and so as superstitions waned, traditions and the dances which accompanied these were forgotten.

The country dances were based on simple steps: runs, walks, skips, hops and so on. The morris dance steps were more complicated and stronger in their jumps. Industrialisation did not stop the 'Dancing

English' completely and in the north the sound of clogs against the cobbles became the basis of a new dance form. One of the dances, the *Lancashire hornpipe*, had very intricate rhythms. Clog dancing even crossed the Atlantic where, joining with other influences, it became known as *Appalachian clog dancing*. This is very popular today, featuring in many festivals and celebrations. It has even returned across the Atlantic in this modified form, where dance groups in Britain complete the chain.

2.3 *'The Tango' from* FAÇADE *(1931) choreography Frederick Ashton. Dancers Margot Fonteyn and Robert Helpmann*

Social dancing has often been used by well-known choreographers. Frederick Ashton's *Façade* starts with a Highland fling and later a polka is danced by a woman who rips her skirt to perform wildly in her bloomers! The work also features a charleston danced by two flappers, four girls waltzing and a mock-passionate tango.

Similarly in his *La Fille Mal Gardée* (*The Unchaperoned Daughter*) there is clogging, maypole dancing and morris dancing. Christopher Bruce, the choreographer of *Sergeant Early's Dream* and *Ghost Dances* uses folk-influenced steps and music. He makes up his own folky steps using influences from tap dance and Irish step dancing mixed with a contemporary style which involves a contracted torso and flexed feet and hands. This is similar to the style of Martha Graham. His dances are often concerned with the lives of communities so the folk influence is very appropriate.

2. Jumping

Every human movement has a preparation, action and recovery phase. This is particularly important in jumping.

2.4 DANCESCAPES (1979) choreography Linda Rickett-Young

Task 5

In pairs, go through the sequence below slowly and continuously three times:

- Bend knees (lift abdominal muscles) — **PREPARATION**
- Extend feet and stretch legs to rise — **ACTION**
- Lower through toe, ball, heel of feet
- Bend knees — **RECOVERY**.

At all times breathe evenly and hold arms by your sides. Where is your focus?

Now repeat it but faster and more suddenly so that it becomes a bouncy jump. **Every landing is a take-off.**

Check that your partner goes through the heel on each landing and stretches legs and feet in the air. Also check the alignment of their torso; are they maintaining a plumb line?

The five types of jumps

- HOP – take-off and land on the same foot;
- LEAP – take-off one foot, land on the other foot;
- JUMP – take-off two feet, land on two feet;
       take-off two feet, land on one foot;
       take-off one foot, land on two feet.

Task 6

1. Do one of the five jumps continuously.
2. Combine it with two others to make a phrase of steps and jumps.

Jumping is an exciting part of dance. In Robert North's *Troy Games* the dancers jump exhaustively. One section, a mock fight for two men, is even performed all on one leg, mostly hopping while using the arms and other leg to gesture. The height of their leaps is breathtaking.

Your aim, as your jumping skills improve, should be to feel a moment when you are suspended in the air, yet still land safely. You can experiment with jumps to falls, turning jumps, different leg gestures and different shapes in the air.

2.5 TROY GAMES *(1974) choreography Robert North for the London
Contemporary Dance Theatre*

3. Turning

There are many types of turn; varying degrees (ie full, less or more);
inward and outward; on and off-balance; while jumping, sitting or lying;
spinning or pivoting and so on.

All these require good placement and a strong sense of centre to avoid
loss of balance. It helps if your eyes focus on where you are headed.
'Spotting' used extensively in ballet, is useful but not essential. Spotting
is fixing the eyes on a point for as long as possible then whipping the
head round as quickly as possible to see the point again. It helps to
avoid dizziness, but it gives a specific look which may not be appropriate
to your choreography.

Turns can start from rising onto a half-toe, or by throwing or swinging
a limb, and they can be performed on various parts of the body; knees,

hips, front of the body, hands, feet etc. Turns make you feel as if your universe is turning around you, and are challenging to perform.

In the mystic dances of the Islamic *Sufi* religion as performed by the Order of the Dancing Dervishes, drums, chanting and flutes accompany endless spinning which gradually accelerates to induce a trance-like state. Such is the power of turning that this type of dance is believed to purify the soul.

4. Gesture

Gestures are movements of parts of the body which do not involve supporting weight. The language of gesture is rich and endless. For example, in Robert North's *Death of a Maiden* he uses the arms to express the blow of death in the back of the woman.

Robert Cohan's *Waterless Method of Swimming Instruction* contains a humorous section where the men use arm gestures to convey the idea of paddling a boat, and hip rotations to add the feel of a playful Latin samba.

Nowhere is gesture used in a more detailed way than in the southern Indian *Kathakali* dance-drama. The hands tell a story and seem to take on a life of their own, reinforced by subtle, powerful facial gestures.

Task 7

Find a painting by Miro or Paul Klee. Using as many different parts of your body as possible, trace the picture. Combine gestures both on the spot and travelling. Use different dynamics to suggest the shapes, colours and textures.

The dance of Lea Anderson for the Cholmondeleys often uses gesture, eg *No Joy* (1987), where the use of sign language creates an atmosphere of darkness as one dancer manipulates another.

5. Stillness

Being still is being active!
Silence in music, space in painting, stillness in dance are all essential to clear expression. In dance stillness often involves balance requiring total control. Stillness can be held on different parts of the body. In order to control a balance on one foot try the following: push down

into the floor through the standing foot, feel your centre pulling up away through the abdominal muscles; feel energy flowing outwards away from your centre to your limbs and back to the centre; hold the stillness. Ensure that your hips and knees are always lined up with the middle of your feet whether in parallel, turn-out or turned in.

Loss of balance will make you fall. Doris Humphrey built a dance technique on the belief that dance occurs in the frightening moment between falling and recovery. As the body shifts its weight it either gives into or resists the pull of gravity and this is felt and sensed expressively.

When you fall it is an intentional 'giving-in' to gravity, but your centre pulls you back and this co-ordination helps to avoid injury. If recovery is instant you will rebound. Avoid landing on knees, elbows, tip of shoulder, hands or tailbone . . . there should be a smooth, successive placing of your body to the floor. Improving your dance technique is one of the best ways of learning how to move correctly and therefore avoid injury.

The feeling of stillness of Monet's painting of a pond of waterlilies is captured in Robert Cohan's *Nymphèas*.

Task 8

Write the five actions on separate pieces of paper, giving each a number between one and five. Close your eyes and pick each piece of paper out in turn and make a phrase in the order that you chose them, ie five jumps followed by two turns etc.

Making dances from individual dance steps in this random fashion is a useful starting point if you are stuck for ideas.

THE WHAT OF DANCE

Through dance technique we learn to manage our bodies efficiently and safely, whilst also meeting new challenges. The centred, flexible strong body can continue the five actions just mentioned in endless ways – the only limit is your imagination.

Your teacher may have taught you a set study by now. Try to pinpoint which actions it uses. Which ones do you find more difficult? Is this because you lose your balance? Which muscles can help you improve your performance? Or perhaps your feet are not working correctly. Try to pinpoint your weaknesses so that you can work to improve them. Finally, try to interpret an overall feel for the set study and give it a title. In this way when you dance it there will be some of yourself in it – after all you are a human being, not a puppet.

Task 9

Choose a phrase or section of a set study and add your own ideas to it. Improvise to find actions which are similar in style and feel to the original.

Further Reading

Cerry, Sandra (1989) *Body and Self: Partners in Movement*, Minton, Human Kinetic Publishers Inc.
Cohan, Robert (1986) *The Dance Workshop*, Unwin.
Frich, Elizabeth (1983) *Matt Mattox Book of Jazz Dance*, Sterling Publishing.
Penrod, James and Gudde, Janice (1970) *The Dancer Prepares*, Plastino, Mayfield Publishing Co.
Sherborn, Elizabeth (1975) *On the Count of One*, Mayfield Publishing Co.

Videos

Ballet Rambert, Different Steps. This gives clear explanations of ballet and Cunningham techniques.

Music

For travelling and jumping: *The Chieftains 3*, Claddagh Records 4CC10.
For combinations of stepping and turns: *K'Jarkas Canto a la muer de mi pueblo*, Tumi C010.
Court Dances of Medieval France, Turnabout, TV34008S.
For relaxation and release: *Dead Can Dance the Serpent's Egg*, CAD C 808.
Ocean Dreams, Dean Evenson, SP7140.

THREE ■ HOW, WHERE, WHEN?

FROM TECHNIQUE TO DANCE

Technical training increases skill and precision. By now you will have learnt a set study and discussed why certain actions may have been chosen. It is obvious that there are other aspects of the movement, not just actions, which had to be selected. Not only the *what* but the *how*, the *where* and the *when*. When composing dance it is vital to select appropriate **dynamics, space** and **time**.

THE HOW – ENERGY (DYNAMICS)

The texture and the colour of dance gives it subtle meanings. Rudolf Laban analysed movement and produced a detailed system of recording movement on paper, known as *Labanotation* which was first published in the 1920s. His theories influenced the growth of modern dance in Europe through his students like Kurt Jooss and Mary Wigman.

Much work in dance education draws on Laban's ideas. He named certain aspects of weight, time, space and flow which can enrich your work:

- **TIME** . . . . . sudden – sustained
- **WEIGHT** . . . firm – light
- **FLOW** . . . . . bound – free
- **SPACE** . . . . . direct – flexible

Certain combinations of these give dance a specific look. For example, the tradition of classical ballet emphasises a sustained carriage of the body and an effortless lightness. This contrasts with the use of the opposites of contraction and release of the spine in the style of Martha Graham which emphasises a 'firmer', more bound, range of energy and a giving into the pull of gravity.

3.1   *Margot Fonteyn as Aurora in* THE SLEEPING PRINCESS *(1939)*

Task 1

Choose one task from the list below and create a short solo in silence.
Use all five actions – travelling, jumping, turning, gesture and stillness
– in your dance.

1. **TIME**: gradually changing from sudden to sustained movement
   compose a solo called 'The river – from source to sea.'
2. **WEIGHT**: quickly changing from firm to light movement, make a
   solo called, 'The rebellion goes up in smoke.'
3. **FLOW**: constantly changing from bound to free and back again,
   produce a solo called, 'The obstacle race.'
4. **SPACE**: using a broom and a piece of silk, create a solo which
   uses direct and flexible movement. Make sure the changes from
   one to the next are a part of the dance.

The terms *energy*, *force*, *dynamics* and *qualities* need to be clarified.

- **energy** is pure potential ever present ready to be used;
- **force** is the intensity of energy being used, ranging from firm to light;
- **dynamics** is force and time combined and results in sudden and sustained.
- **efforts** which we see as named by Rudolf Laban. Thrust, flick, press, float, dab, glide, slash and wring arise from how the energy is applied, either directly or indirectly.

You can use a wide range of dynamics to produce many different qualities and expressions, for example:

- **swinging** – a heavy drop followed by a light suspension, appears free and natural.
- **vibrate** – sudden repeated percussive movements appear as a quiver, shake or tremble.
- **percussive** – sharp, sudden, direct impulses, eg strike, thrust, punch.
- **suspended** – breathless, weightless, soaring, eg at the top of a leap or balance;
- **collapse** – a total giving in to gravity, eg slow sink or fast fall which does not rebound.

Task 2

Divide the floor into a grid of four or six areas (chalk marks will do). As a group, allocate a landscape to each area, eg a strong gusty wind, a dark cave where spiders' webs brush your face as you walk, a floor covered with drawing pins, deep sticky mud, a thick jungle which you have to hack your way through, an earthquake etc. Make up some of your own. Travel around the room finding your own route and making clear changes in the dynamics and qualities with which you move from one area to another. When everyone has established their routes, try mixing and matching various couples or trios to see how they look together. Sometimes you may chance to find some which look interesting together – either because of their similarities or their contrasts.

Each movement quality invokes a general feeling and when a number are used together they convey more general meanings, feelings and sensations.

In Robert Cohan's *Waterless Method of Swimming Instruction* he uses a great deal of sustainment and suspension to give the impression of floating in water.

Christopher Bruce chooses powerful, strong intense qualities for the ghosts in *Ghost Dances*. These menaces loom over the livelier, light folk steps of the mortal world which in turn are transformed into deathly, slow sustained walking steps after their violent deaths. The three contrasting qualities confront us, the audience, with the needless taking of life in the violent regimes of South America.

Tom Jobe's *Liquid Assets* takes its ideas from a time when Jobe lived in New York and worked to save money to fund his training at London Contemporary Dance School. He describes his work in an office and how he differed from the other office workers, being more laid back and yet business-like. The others gave the impression of being prim and proper but often spend their time gossiping. In his 'dancing spaghetti' style the soloists' free flexible movement contrasts with the more bound, direct 'uptight' manner of the other dancers.

THE WHERE – SPACE

'I looked to space as a potential three-dimensional canvas'
Alwin Nikolais[1]

Designing dance in space is essential. The way in which movement and dancers are positioned must be appropriately chosen to make the expression of the dance clear. Space is alive in dance. It is like an invisible partner: it can surround you, pulsate, be an opponent to be pushed away.

In ballet, design in space can be pure visual delight for its own sake.

[1]Nikolais, Alwin (1979), *Vision of Modern Dance*, ed. Jean Morrison Brown, p. 116.

3.2 WATERLESS METHOD OF SWIMMING INSTRUCTION (1974) *choreography Robert Cohan for the London Contemporary Dance Theatre*

3.3 LIQUID ASSETS (1985) *choreography Tom Jobe for the London Contemporary Dance Theatre*

Mary Wigman, an early German modern dancer, would use space as an active element. If we are to understand how she did this, and indeed to make use of space in this way, we must break down space into its components.

Personal Space and General Space

Siobahn Davies's *New Galileo* (LCDT 1984) begins with small movements which gradually enlarge to fill the stage. This is a clear example of using the extremes of personal and general space to make a statement. In everyday life we carry our own private 'space bubble' with us and feel uncomfortable if someone invades this by coming too close, but in dancing we break the usual space distance rules for visual or dramatic impact.

In Glen Tetley's *Embrace Tiger and Return to Mountain* (Rambert 1968), the opening section fills the stage with dancers placed space bubble distance apart as they go through their ritual *T'ai chi* meditations. Even though they are separate in space and time their identical movement phrases create a strong feeling of unity and strength. Later, duets bring the dancers very close to each other with a great deal of touch and shadowing. We sense their agitation as their bubbles are invaded.

3.4 *EMBRACE TIGER AND RETURN TO MOUNTAIN (1968) choreography Glen Tetley*

Task 3

SHADOWS. In twos, one leads the other and becomes a second skin – as close as possible. Travel, change level. As the sun sinks the shadow lengthens and moves further away. You still feel connected even though the space is between you. Change roles through a smooth natural transition.

3.5 Tightrope Dance Company (1980) choreography Linda Rickett-Young

Level

In early modern dance techniques like that of Martha Graham, a low earthy feel was emphasised as a reaction against the verticality and constant lift of classical ballet. The middle or medium level is our everyday 'feet on the ground' state. It is from here that we explore the possibilities of using all three levels, high, medium and low, in their extremes; falling, jumping and lifting each other.

Robert Cohan's use of the ladder in *Hunter of Angels* illustrates well the use of levels to reinforce the images of heaven, earth and hell in the struggle between twins Jacob and Esau and the angel.

Task 4

The whole group start outside the space with a variety of musical/percussion instruments. These are played in response to the movement and dancers may respond to the sounds.

1. In your own time, dancers run into the space and fall, quickly rise without stopping and continue or exit.
2. As for (1) but very slowly with stillness on low levels.
3. Combine (1) and (2) and relate to the other dancers by echoing, shadowing, matching and mirroring them.
4. Travel into the space on a high level to take a still shape on a high, low or medium level and exit immediately. Emphasise shapes which respond to dancers already in the space, ie either copy, complement or contrast. Try to travel in many different ways.
5. Repeat (4) but include chairs, boxes, platforms etc and contact between dancers, eg assist a jump, help up from a fall and so on.

Direction, Dimension and Plane

Some images are expressed through **direction**, eg a backward retreat, a forward chase or race, uncertain sideways sidling. See the contrast between groups of dancers making up strident, marching armies and those forming solemn processions of fearful slaves.

Dimensions are the result of joining two directions:

- **Depth** – forward and backward; advance and retreat
- **Width** – side to side; open and close
- **Height** – up and down; rise and sink.

Planes are the result of joining two dimensions:

- **Vertical** – height and width
- **Horizontal** – width and depth
- **Sagittal** – depth and height.

3.6 *SODA LAKE (1981) choreography Richard Alston*

Task 5

Egyptian Frieze. Within large groups – one person takes a shape emphasising the vertical plane in two dimensions, height and width. People join in one at a time in response to the design as it grows, ie varying level, closeness etc.

Compose a solo dance called 'The Amazing Moving One-legged Table' emphasising the horizontal plane.

Interesting examples of the use of direction, dimension and planes can be found in *Soda Lake* by Richard Alston (1981) and Martha Graham's *Frontier* (1935).

Soda Lake was a solo for Michael Clark performed in silence. It takes the theme of a vast American landscape as seen through the eyes of sculptor Nigel Hall. The dance relates to the sculpture in stillness, direction and shape. Patterns on the floor and in the air are clearly seen.

For example, a circular pattern which Alston calls 'tracing the shapes' echoes the suspended hoop as are the movements which shadow the vertical pole.

Alston started his training with London Contemporary Dance School and so would have worked in the Graham style. Interestingly, Martha Graham's solo *Frontier* uses a simple set designed by Isamu Noguchi which consists of two ropes and a fence, putting the dancer in the vast American wild west. She said it '. . . has to do with plains, the distances, the vista. It's about roads that disappear into the distances or a railroad track.' It uses simple movements like rising and sinking, forward advances, travelling with large circular gestures in the air, opening and closing and small flexible twists. The isolation of the lone woman on her ranch miles from anywhere is expressed clearly and strongly.

Shape, Space Patterns

The shape of movement in space can make patterns:
1. in the air;
2. on the floor (curved, straight or angular); or
3. as the overall body shape (symmetrical of asymmetrical).

Air pattern: curved, circular, flowing graceful and lyrical can be felt as soft, caring, reflective, soothing and natural. Straight, sharply angular tend to imply mechanistic, imposing, aggressive themes.

Floor pattern: similarly our path in space has similar implications. Circles can be powerful symbols of unification of people, as in folk dances, and this feeling can be communicated to an audience. Geometric floor patterns create interest through sudden changes of direction.

Task 6

1. List images, dramatic ideas, characters that seem to match the standard patterns below and others which would be more appropriate to the free forms, eg 0 = together we stand.

Standard   Free Form

2. Choose one of each type of pattern and travel along it on the floor, first with similar body shapes and air patterns, then with contrasting ones. How does this feel and what are the possible ways it changes the expression?

Symmetrical or asymmetrical: *Symmetry*, ie the same both sides, produces feelings of stability, control and authority. *Asymmetry* produces tension, unpredictability and contrast. In dance one can be used to emphasise the other. Too much of either one can be monotonous.

Task 7

The Robot. In pairs, imagine one of you is a prototype robot and the other is operating you by remote control, but you can only move asymmetrically. The operator calls out body parts and instructions such as *sit, lie down on your front side or back, stand, travel*, etc.

Discuss how this felt. What does it tell you about human movement? What felt difficult and why?

In Cohan's *Hunter of Angels*, symmetry of the duo's body shapes in mirroring is used to show the relationship of the twin brothers.

In 1912 Vaslav Nijinsky set new standards in classical ballet technique with his high leaps, but he also shocked audiences with a revolutionary choreography, as in the ballet *L'Après Midi d'un Faune*. To music by Debussy and design by Leon Bakst the influence of Greek friezes on the movement broke all the traditional rules of ballet. Limbs were held parallel to give a flat look as in figures portrayed on Greek vases. This new look combined with sexuality and disregard for the music's rhythms shocked Parisian audiences and earned Nijinsky the title of the first 'modern choreographer'.

Focus

The eyes are the windows to the soul and there is great expressive power in a dancer's gaze. Do we want the audience to feel that the dancers are escaping from, drawn to, sharing with something or someone? Performers can create dramatic and emotional effects with their focus.

3.7 *L'APRÈS MIDI D'UN FAUNE (1912) choreography Vaslav Nijinsky*

3.8 *THE MAD BAD LINE (1990) choreography Linda Rickett-Young for BAD Dance Company*

Yvonne Rainer, however, considered this as artificial enhancement of the dance and in *Trio A* (1966) she deliberately never let the dancers' focus confront the audience. This was a part of the post modern dance revolutionary attitude, that of dance as a collective, democratic activity rather than one of elitist values, as they saw in the work of earlier dancers like Graham.

'No to spectacle, no to virtuosity, no to transformation and magic and makebelieve.' This statement by Rainer is a good example of how dance was evolving and reflecting the liberal social values of the 1960s.

The term *facing* means the focus of the body in relation to the movement. This could be in line with, away from or in many different directions from the movement. Facing is important when deciding how to position a movement in order to see it most clearly in terms of its design, ie from the side, front, back or diagonal.

When dancing the focus may be on a part of the body, the walls, the far distance. Whatever is chosen, the dancer must be aware of the need to draw attention to the movement's intention. For example, how would you organise the focus and facings in a theme such as a tennis match?

Task 8

In pairs, create a short, simple step pattern of 12 counts. Take turns to do it varying

1. the focus of the face and
2. the direction and facings.

Describe to each other the different effects this makes, which effects are more successful and why.

In Robert North's *Death and the Maiden* the female's focus is continually drawn towards the figure of death. She seems tormented and haunted because wherever she looks she sees death and there is no escape.

The Stage Space

Do dancers control the space or does the space control the dance? Traditional ballet choreographers – and some modern dance ones too – use the stage space according to set criteria of staging such as the strength of the centre spot and of the diagonal from upstage right to downstage left. Not all choreographers use this method. Merce Cunningham ignored it in favour of treating all areas as equal and leaving the audience to decide what to look at first. In his dance *Tread* (1970), lines of electric fans on poles divide the space at the front of the stage. The audience chooses either to watch the spaces between the poles, or how one dancer passes between and around them, or the entire stage.

Some general rules about the stage space:

1. Stage right and left are from the performer's position. For the audience it is the other way round.
2. Traditionally, centre stage is the most powerful place and the upstage right to downstage left diagonal is the strongest.
3. Action at the front tends to be more humorous.
4. Action at the back tends to be more distant in space and time.

As already stated this conventional theatrical style was experimented with

3.9 TREAD (1970) *choreography Merce Cunningham*

3.10 MY SEX OUR DANCE (1987) *choreography Lloyd Newson for DV8*

in the 1960s and 70s. Rosemary Butcher, after working in New York in the 70s, set her dances on beaches, mountains and in art galleries. More recently video and TV have influenced dance and pieces are written especially for this medium, the modern technology producing rich and spectacular interplay of movement and space. Butcher's work *Touch the Earth* was filmed in 1988 in an abandoned warehouse. Lloyd Newson's daring *My Sex Our Dance* has also been adapted for video (1987).

Task 9

1. Create a dance in the round called 'Circle Ritual'.
2. Discuss the various spaces which you are familiar with and that the whole or part of the group may improvise in, eg a playground, a beach, a weights room, a corridor, a garden, a football pitch etc. Be aware of all the different sights and sounds that may affect your movement. Decide where the audience might be.

You can choose how to use space to convey your ideas most advantageously. The possibilities are endless – make sure you do not lose your way!

THE WHEN – TIME AND RHYTHM

Time is passing us every day. We sense it through a *pulse*, ie a section of set length that marks rhythm and gives it order. As a dancer you must be able to keep time accurately. The sense of rhythm often determines dance styles such as Jazz, Indian, Afro-Carribean or Flamenco.

Pulse and Tempo

The pulse of a heart beat is a sign of life and measures time, ie passing. It underlies all our movements. Pulse can vary in speed. Five minutes of a movement at a slow tempo can seem longer than five minutes of a movement at a fast tempo.

Task 10

One person times one minute on a stopwatch for the group. They move as slowly as possible for what they estimate is a minute. They must stop when they think a minute is up, however long it takes. Repeat with fast movement. How accurate was their estimate? How different did the two tempi feel?

A slow, leisurely waltz feels and looks smooth and lyrical unlike a fast one which is animated and lively. Speed or tempo affects the mood, feeling or quality of a dance.

Acceleration is a gradual increase in tempo; *Deceleration* is a gradual decrease in tempo. You can build interest by increasing tempo in strength and size, like crescendos in music. Similarly, quieter sections can be made to emphasise softer, deeper, smaller moments. The contrast of these two builds sections in the dance, giving overall pace and form.

In Robert North's *Death and the Maiden* the tempo increases and decreases of Schubert's music are reflected in the moments of dramatic intensity and the sections building up to them. The maiden dances frantically around the space to a particular section of fast music, hopelessly meeting death at every turn, unable to escape her fate.

Accent

An accent in rhythm is a stress on one or more beats. Try clapping the following, accenting the clap marked v:

v́2345678/v́2345678/v́234/v́234/v́2/v́2/v́v́34

34 indicates to clap the off-beat. Now try the above in movement, say with opening and closing, rising and sinking or walking with changes of direction. Accents can shift to create surprise, or, if spaced further apart, give a solemn dignified mood. Conversely if accents occur close together a more vivacious, urgent mood is achieved.

Task 11

Try to create a phrase of six triplets where the accent is always shifting from one to two to three in an unexpected order. Be clear how you create the accent, eg clap or tilt the torso suddenly; make an arm gesture; change level etc.

Metrical Rhythm

In most western music, phrases of beats are divided into measures occurring at regular intervals. The number of beats in a measure is the *metre* and this gives regular timing to support, play off or contrast against the movement. The top part of a time signature shows how many beats form a measure and the bottom number indicates the kind of note that receives one count;

2/4: indicates two beats in a measure and one quarter note receives one count.

Some movements fit more naturally into certain metres, for example regular swings fit usually in a 6/8 metre. Some metres are uneven and produce moods of comedy or tension in their asymmetry:

5/4 1̌2̌345 or 1̌234̌5
7/4 1̌234̌567 or 1̌234̌5̌67

When using strictly metered music, beware of letting the music dictate the rhythm. You can avoid this by accenting movement which clashes with the musical accent. Use different accents for different dancers. When the accent shifts to a usually *un*accented beat (*syncopation*) it can create a very exciting effect, especially if different dancers are syncopated against each other and the music. Similarly, more random movement creates rhythmical and visual tension.

Many choreographers show clear use of music and rhythmical styles. Richard Alston in *Dealing with Shadows* uses the sonata form of the music by Mozart. Alston's indisputable musicality also reflects the natural rhythms and qualities of his dancers.

In Robert North's *Troy Games*, breath rhythms give the movement its shape as well as the complex meters of the Brazilian *batacuda* music.

Afro-Caribbean dancing is one of the styles in which rhythm is all-important. Dance and drumming go together in African culture. Several rhythms are played simultaneously, creating a complex blend to which the dancers respond when called by the master drummer.

Task 12

In a trio play the complex rhythm below on three different drums at the same time.

	1	2	3	4	5	6	7	8	9	10	11	12
A	1			4	5		7			10		
B		2	3		5	6		8		10		
C	1		3		5		7		9	10	11	12

accent where the numbers show, play softly in the blanks

You can experiment with this, adding more instruments etc. Drums and songs are often used to accompany rhythmic work movements such as digging, laying railway tracks, bringing water etc.

Task 13

Walk in pairs to a moderate pulse. One dancer keeps the pulse while the other person walks, skips or takes any simple steps in double time. The person walking allows the other to keep up by changing length of stride, or floor pattern or direction.

Repeat, this time trying to establish a more interesting phrase of steps which is repeatable and keeps up with the walking partner.

In Task 13 we see a regular beat as supporting the less regular one. Regular beats such as a comforting, cradle-like rock, or a relaxing, hypnotic waltz can help to keep timing organised. When the beat becomes irregular it can be more difficult to organise but it is fun and challenging. It gives dance movement an element of surprise or shock, comic effect or irritation. Music from the far east can often sound discordant to us because of its different sense of rhythmic organisation. Try listening to some Balinese *gamelan* music – it would be an interesting source of accompaniment for your own dance compositions.

Nonmetrical Rhythms

Rhythm is all around you: in the sea, in your body (your heartbeat, breathing, walking) in machinery, in animals. Often these do not have a regular pulse but may speed up or slow down quite unpredictably. Dance movement sometimes has its own nonmetrical rhythm which may only relate to music by broadly going across the beat and can be performed in silence or with the accompaniment of breathing, stamping, clapping. These natural rhythms are just as strong as the more planned metric ones and are a vast treasure for the choreographer.

Task 14

1. Try to move continually falling (breathing in) and rising (breathing out) and vice versa. Discuss how different these actions feel.
2. Repeat (1) with wavelike movements, opening and closing, swinging.
3. Put together a solo where the breath leads and shapes the movement.
4. In threes, improvise with action and reaction using different sorts of breaths, eg sigh, blow, gasp. Form a short duet with a 'question and answer' structure.

In Glen Tetley's *Pierrot Lunaire* (1962), he is influenced by the structure of the Schoenberg score of the same name. A characteristic of Schoenberg's score is that, unlike more conventional works, it does not have many long phrases or much repetition. There are extremes of sudden, fast tempos which disappear into slow sections and broken rhythms. As with the random, chance procedures of Cunningham's dance to music by John Cage in the early 1950s, the results are more like natural, spontaneous and non-metric rhythms than more metered ones.

Further Reading

Cheyney and Strader (1975) *Modern Dance*, Allyn and Baker Inc.
Ellfeldt, Lois (1974) *A Primer for Choreographers*, Dance Books.

Videos

Soda Lake, Richard Alston for Rambert Dance Company, National Resource Centre for Dance production. Clear explanation of Alston's choice of movement in relation to the sculpture. Describes how he uses aspects of space, dynamics and action.

Music

Task 1 – *The Mission*, Ennio Morricone, Virgin (1986).
> *Music for Dance 3*, Chris Benstead, PO Box 727, London SE13 3DX.
> *Music For Instruments and Electronic Sounds*, Donald, Erb Nonesuch H 71223.

Task 5 – *Penguin Café Orchestra*, Broadcasting from Home, Virgin EGEDC 38.

Tasks 7, 8 – Tracks 2 and 4 from Dance Technic available from D W S Harry, Primrose Studios, Lancaster.

FOUR ■ FINDING, CHOOSING, SHAPING

While building your technical competence and understanding of dynamics, time and space you will often find yourself improvising, exploring movement, trying out new ideas, as in some of the earlier tasks. Set aside time to use your own starting-points and find your own style. Your imagination is a special source by which ideas are chosen, movements selected, and gives the final dance its own unique individual style.

By now you could probably tell the difference between choreography by Martha Graham and Merce Cunningham, both of whom have their own internal style. They do not imitate reality, nor do they rely on personal mannerisms but select the movements which are most suited to express their ideas. By exaggerating, diminishing, distorting and abstracting personal statements they stylise and crystalise the original stimulus. You must learn to trust and follow your insights and ideas.

STIMULUS, IMPROVISATION, ABSTRACTION

'You are your own master and student. There is no value in copying what someone else has done. You must search within your own body. What you discover there will be for your own benefit.'

Hanya Holm[1]

Once the basic tools are available you can begin to use your instrument to make new movement: at this stage solo work is appropriate. Use starting points which are of interest to you. Do you like poetry? Try to use a poem as a springboard for movement ideas. Do you keep a diary? Take a day from it and create movement from the events and feelings of that day. Do you have a strong belief in something? Can you express this in movement?

Such starting points or stimuli can be drawn from any aspect of life. They may be very clear, even from the start; begin as a vague hint or

[1]Hanya Holm, *Vision of Modern Dance* (1979). ed, Jean Morrison Brown, Dance Books, p71.

60

even change completely during improvisation. Sometimes the starting point can be the dance itself. A student of mine based a project on The Kosh Dance Company's production of *Dinner Dance*. After attending the performance and a workshop she focused on their use of stories about human relationships and their use of words. She wrote a poem and composed a solo dance based on it. Here is the poem.

VOICES FROM THE AIR

Loneliness, confusion and fear
Only the cold air seems near
Only the cold wind to hear
And images in the night to conquer my fear.

I run, I walk,
I fall, I stalk,
Like an owlet in the night
Forever and ever will I fight.

I fight until it's right
In the middle of the night
The door opens
And dawn breaks
Free at last
Goodbye to the past
Goodbye to the monster that was me.

Marilyn Zaloumis Prior

The final solo was not a copy of the original Kosh dance but became an interesting and imaginative dance with a life of its own.

Paul Taylor said

'I don't know where ideas come from. If I waited for inspiration I'd never get anything done . . . I just get busy in the studio and sometimes when I start I haven't got a clue what we're going to do. I just start. If it doesn't lead anywhere, then I start over . . . There's no lack of ideas; it's harder to eliminate them and get what you want.'[1]

[1]Paul Taylor, *Quintet: 5 American Dance Companies* (1972), Maria Hodgson, Macmillan, New York, p72.

During improvisation you allow your body and mind to follow freely along an idea and try not to worry too much about technique. Try out things for the first time, be spontaneous. Eventually you will realise that there is as much skill in learning to improvise as there is in learning technique. Letting go is not always easy. Try to be totally involved with the movement and this will help you to be less inhibited.

As you throw away material, what is left is a more focused expression of the original stimulus, and often the ideas and movements change as you work. Anna Sokolow describes how in *Rooms* she 'wanted to do something about people in a big city. The theme of loneliness and non-communication evolved as I worked . . .' and in *Dreams*, which was her condemnation of Nazi Germany, when she started she . . . 'only had the idea of dreams, but they became nightmares and then I saw they were related to the concentration camps. Once this happened I intensified the theme by focusing on it.'[2]

Improvisation has long been a strong influence in the world of theatre. In many ancient dance traditions such as Indian dance and Flamenco it is a much admired and respected skill. The dancers play with the intricate cross-rhythms which results in brilliant cascades of steps and sounds. Traditional western theatre tended to gradually discard improvisation in favour of more rigid rules of presentation. This is particularly noticeable in classical ballet, where the role of choreographer is one of ultimate responsibility for the dancers being in a certain place at a certain moment within the frame of the proscenium stage. The work of Isadora Duncan, on the other hand, was based on freedom of choice of movement during the performance. After several years of formal approaches such as those of Martha Graham, in the 1940s and 1950s Merce Cunningham and composer John Cage reintroduced improvisation as a main component of choreography and performance. In their work both dancers and audience were given choices of what to do or what to look at.

In the 1960s this was developed still further in New York by such dancers as Anna Halprin, Steve Paxton, Douglas Dunn and Yvonne Rainer. They questioned every aspect of form to include improvisation in performance and audience participation and gradually it became popular not only to watch dance but also to join in. Companies such as Motionhouse in Britain use improvisation in their performances and

[2]Anna Sokolow, *Vision of Modern Dance*, p110.

4.1 *Isadora Duncan*

in their work with people who have special needs. Improvisation is also widely used in dance therapy.

Improvisation is a way of finding new ways of moving so that you are not always producing the same ideas. From whatever your stimulus is, try to react spontaneously to it and start to make choices from the fragments which you feel work best. You will need to concentrate deeply, as often movements which are successful are also instantly forgotten! Treat this not as a source of frustration, however, but rather one of fun and magic.

Task 1

Choose from the list of stimuli below and see how much different movement material you can think up in five minutes.

1. Electronic music
2. A wall of the studio
3. A piece of clothing
4. A photo.

Now the movement material will begin to be more clearly shaped into phrases which have a beginning, middle and end. Like a sentence it starts to make sense, to have a kind of movement logic with an overall form and feeling.

You will find that phrases vary in length and this helps to create interest. They also reveal ideas, impressions and design which tell us more about the original stimulus. This is achieved by a process called *abstraction*.

Task 2

Watch an extract of dance on video from a favourite choreographer and try to spot the phrases.

Abstraction reduces an idea or image, say anger, to its most basic form. It does not copy reality but throws away some information and takes a close-up look at one small element of it which hits hard at the audience.

Often they respond with a gut reaction to this intense, larger-than-life image.

Dance uses abstraction to deal with a wide range of subjects, from the highly emotional, such as Christopher Bruce's *Ghost Dances* to the fantastic images of Alwin Nikolais to the cool movement of Merce Cunningham. When the focus is on *pure* movement or design, dance is more abstract, with concern for time, rhythm and shape rather than plot, emotion or character. Balanchine's *Agon* (Stravinsky) is a clear example of this, with its focus on rhythmic invention, arrangement, shape and placement of dancers.

In the ballet *Agon* by George Balanchine the movement is based on the music by Stravinsky which uses the stimulus of 16th and 17th century court dances like the Galliard. Both composer and choreographer give the classical style a more modern, sharper feel so that the title *Agon* (Greek for contest), is really the challenge to the audience. They expect a classical style but, as the dancers perform in a playful competition with each other they are presented with an abstract toughness. The usual classical *pas de deux* is distorted so that the man slides around the woman on the floor in order to promenade her around, rather than the other way round. This powerful twist surprises the audience. This is an example of abstracting from a movement stimulus to create a pure dance style.

But dance is one of the least abstract arts because of the presence of the human figure. For example, if your stimulus was an image of a family, let us call them the McNormals, you may use their relationships to suggest ideas for movement. You may then create a fantasy situation, say the adolescent daughter is really an alien from another planet who takes on bizarre ways of moving, eg she levitates, melts, explodes. You are selecting *aspects* of an image. Cunningham's *Travelogue* is a fine example of using images of animal movement to abstract a rich range of phrases. The fact that it is performed by human figures allows it to stand by and for itself, without the performers feeling that they are pretending to be animals.

The well-known 'be a tree', is not so silly as it may at first appear. If movement is the starting point and appropriately interesting movements are selected then a dance can be composed successfully.

4.2   THE MAD BAD LINE, THE McNORMAL FAMILY (1990) choreography Linda Rickett-Young for BAD Dance Company

Task 3

Take the theme of the Amazon Rainforest and improvise around it to produce a rich range of images, ideas and movements. The many birds and animals of the forest floor and the high canopy of the tree-tops; the lives of the Indian tribes; their agriculture, myths and legends. From these many images create a dance for a large group which has many sections. Make sure each small group chooses only one idea. In order to structure the whole dance, allow groups to come and go as and when they feel it is appropriate. Gradually decide on an order by drawing on your observations of what works best.

'Improvisations require different styles of thought at different moments in their evolution. A dialogue between wildness and order.'[1]

[1]Miranda Tufnell and Chris Crickmay, *Body, Space, Image.*

4.3 *South Asian Bharatanatyam dance*

4.4 *Laurie Booth and Company*

4.5 *Frederick Ashton as Pierrot in*
CARNIVAL *(1935). Notice the contrasting
looks of these different dance styles*

STYLE

During the process of shaping phrases you will find everyone has their own special way of picking a stimulus and arranging the movement. This gives dance individual style. You would not confuse the music of Stravinsky with that of Debussy or Bob Marley, or the fashion designer Christian Dior with Katherine Hamnett. So it is in dance. Style is a part of everyday life: our hair, clothes, food, speech. We choose to suit our taste, but often this choice is *modified* because we do not want to appear too different from everyone else. In all arts, choice emphasises important differences, exaggerates and distorts. No two people are the same and so their styles of movement will differ. To make this clearer let us recap on dance history, which was covered in more detail in Chapter 1.

Occasionally a new style arises as a result of a strong creative individual's innovative techniques and procedures. Indeed, modern dance in the twentieth century has grown from this. As we discussed in Chapter 2, Nijinsky's ballets such as *L'Après Midi d'un Faune*, (Debussy) used flat, frieze-like parallel movement inspired from Greek art and erotic gestures. Although this scandalised and shocked the audiences of the time, retrospectively he is regarded as a pioneer of modern dance.

Similarly the work of Isadora Duncan, Graham and Cunningham has influenced the progress of dance history. The more you know about different styles the more your own work will be supported. For example, if you were working on a dance which was simple, direct and emphasised rhythm, some study of African dance would be helpful. (See also Chapter 3 pp 56–57).

African music and dance travelled the world with the slave trade and developed into new styles in various countries by blending with European traditions. In this way dance styles such as tap, jazz, Latin, disco, street dance have grown. Tom Jobe in his fast moving *Rite Elektrik* set in the night world of clubland used references to disco and street dance styles.

In the world of visual art and music certain styles became associated with schools, each defined by its own way of seeing reality. These five schools may be useful to know about when shaping movement.

These were:

- Realism
- Expressionism
- Impressionism
- Cubism
- Surrealism.

Realism

Realism attempts to reproduce 'things as they are' but this will always be influenced by the artist's personality. It does not avoid selection. A full-length drama as in Ashton's *Month in the Country* presents a story as seen through a poet's eyes.

Expressionism

This attempts to portray an intense, emotional view of the world. The work of the early modern dancers in Europe such as Mary Wigman was highly emotional. *The Green Table* (1932) by Kurt Jooss shows the horrors of war and death while greedy politicians argue around a green conference table. They bargain about the lives of ordinary people as if it were a game of snooker. The masks they wear and the skeleton figure of death make the sinister treachery even more scary, strongly expressionist and emotionally-charged.

Impressionism

Impressionism gives a suggestion of the real world. Robert Cohan's *Forest* and *Nymphèas* both offer changing mood and atmosphere rather than realistic images of the scene's animals or birds etc. In *Nymphèas* he takes as his stimulus the Impressionist painting of waterlilies by Monet.

Cubism

This arranges shapes in surprising ways so that things can be seen from all sides at once. In 1917 Leonarde Massine created *Parade* for the Ballets Russes and even though the dance itself was not cubist it was an early attempt to experiment. Picasso, the father of Cubist painting, designed

4.6 NYMPHÈAS (1976) choreography Robert Cohan for the London Contemporary Dance Theatre

4.7 The Cholmondeleys in COLD SWEAT by Lea Anderson

the set and costumes. The effect was so stunning that it almost swamped the dance. Satie's music was a mixture of jazz, popular music and real sounds such as pistol shots and this, combined with the ballet's images of early cinema (Charlie Chaplin, cowboys and villains), Chinese magic and Ragtime produced a truly radical, if not completely successful, production. Later in the 1960s the post modern dance style addressed such cubist issues as the angle of presentation of dancers and the juxtaposition of the unexpected.

Surrealism

Surrealism distorts reality by taking things out of their usual setting, creating an impact of absurdity, dreamlike and unlikely. The work of Lea Anderson of the Cholmondeleys can often appear surreal in its use of quirky gesture.

A healthy respect and curiosity for different techniques, theories of movement, cultural and historical styles can remind you that you are a unique artist, and can be a source of reference to broaden your style as it grows.

Task 4

Choose a choreographer and find photos, film and writings from which to identify the style. Now improvise in that style using appropriate music, theme, props etc. Select and shape phrases to produce a short study (max two mins.)

This task may make you move in ways which feel odd to you, but it is important to realise that your personal style is *more* than what you think is typical of you. This is freeing you from your self-imposed limits and teaching you to make the best use of them. It is also pinpointing your weaknesses so that you know what to improve. Personal style is about learning to be versatile.

Task 5

By now you may have choreographed a solo. Discuss with others what makes yours special. Here is a check list of some movements which they might see:

- Travelling or staying on the spot or in a certain direction;
- Steady or impulsive;
- Gestural or whole body movement;
- Liquid or percussive;
- On a certain level and so on.

Use this discussion to learn about your strengths and weaknesses. A follow-up which you may find interesting is to compose for someone else using their own personal style.

It is not every day that a Fokine is born, but what is important is to understand that you are special and that your thoughts, ideas and imagination are just as good as anyone elses. I will leave the final words to the famous:

'With every new ballet that I produce I seek to empty myself of some plastic obsession and every ballet I do is for me solving a balletic problem.'

Frederick Ashton[1]

'The exponent of modern dancing has to fight two things. One is the belief that it simply means self-expression and the other is that no technique is required.'

Martha Graham[2]

'I do everything I know how in dance.'

Twyla Tharp[3]

[1]Frederick Ashton in *Dance from Magic to Art* (1976), William C. Brown and Co, Lois Ellfeldt, p205.
[2]Martha Graham in *Dance from Magic to Art* (1976), William C. Brown and Co.
[3]Twyla Tharp, op cit.

Further Reading

Horst, Louis and Russell, Carol (1973) *Modern Dance Forms*, Dance Horizons.
Morganroth, Joyce (1987) *Dance Improvisation*, University of Pittsburgh Press
Steinman, Louise (1986) *The Knowing Body*, Shambhala.
Tufnell and Crickmay (1990) *Body, Space, Image*, Virago Press.

Video

Different Dancers Similar Motion, Motionhouse, Oxford Independent Video 1990.

Music

Task 1 – Electronomusic 9 Images, John Pfeiffer, Victrola VICS 1371 RCA.
Task 3 – *Spirit of the Rainforest*, Terry Oldfield, New World NWC 195.

Music useful for improvisation:

Andy Sheppard, *Introductions in the Dark*, Antilles anc. 8742.
Gassman, *Electronic Music for the Ballet*, Westminster WG8110.

FIVE ■ DANCE COMPOSITION

FORMING AND FORM

'The work as a whole must be of one stuff, as an emerald is all emerald – crush it to powder and each tiny pinch of that powder will still be an emerald.'

Ted Shawn[1]

All arts arrange their elements in an orderly way with meaning and purpose, whether organising the notes of music or the plot of a novel. This process gives *form* and it is as basic to life itself as it is to art. It is seen in the growth of a tree, the rising and setting of the sun, the cycle of the seasons. Art uses form to help an idea grow, to support it and to give it structure. It is the life within the dance which has grown naturally from the stimulus, through improvisation and the shaping of phrases. In dance, it is up to us to decide an appropriate order for the phrases and all the components. In this way, phrases build up into larger units, forming *sequences*. These sequences need to be logically developed so that they have a beginning, middle and end.

FORMING THE MOVEMENT

Devices for dance composition

These are not tricks of the trade but ways to make more out of less, yet remaining within an overall plan.

1.1. **Motif:** the shaped phrases of movement are known as *motifs* and they contain the style and images of the dance. They are repeated, developed and varied so give the overall shape and expression (think about the emerald).

2.2. **Motif development:** Motifs can be danced back to front, upside-down, be split up into smaller parts, with each part then used separately

[1]Ted Shawn, *Vision of Modern Dance*, p30.

or in a different order or combined with other motifs. Below is a list of ways in which motifs can be developed.

- Repetition;
- Using different parts of the body;
- Making the motif larger or smaller;
- By adding to or changing the actions;
- Performing it on a different level;
- Altering the focus;
- Changing the direction, dimension or plane;
- Redesigning the floor or air pattern;
- With increased or decreased tempo;
- Varied rhythm;
- Changing the accents;
- Performed backwards;
- Turning the body upside-down;
- Altering the quality;
- Changing the amount of force;
- Fragmenting the motif;
- A combination of any of the above.

Task 1

The motif and nothing but the motif!

Create a motif. Develop it in all the ways listed above. Some will work better than others. Choose eight of them and make a complete study in which the motif appears in its pure form at least three times. Now, in pairs, discuss how well the dance works. Does it hold your interest? Did it have any unrelated movement?

Motif development is a way of producing a lot of movement and although it will alter the look of the dance the overall logic will not be lost. It also helps avoid being stuck for ideas!

2. Motif Variation: when a motif is developed it can result in any number of different movements, but when it is varied the order of the movements within it is constant. Therefore the motif must be interesting enough in the first place to avoid the boredom of too much repetition.

Task 2

A group of four people are to compose a motif. Each one of you varies it by changing the mood, eg lyrically, sneakily, nervously, melo-dramatically. Perform the motif for the rest of the class first together then taking each variation in turn.

A fine example of this is Doris Humphrey's *Water Study* (1928) in which the curve of the dancers' backs are wavelike and the increase in force sweeps them across the stage then fades again to leave them in stillness.

Another example is David Gordon's *Chair* (1974). A movement motif danced in, on, over, under, around and through a chair is repeated five times with variation in direction, tempo and accompaniment.

3. Transition: within the individual motifs and in between the motifs, sequences and sections of the dance there must be natural links known as *transitions*. These transitions can vary in complexity. They can be gradual or sudden, they can overlap. Above all they must not be allowed to hide the material of the main movement.

Robert Cohan's *Waterless Method of Swimming Instruction* uses the simple idea of entries and exits from the pool to link the sections of the dance fluently. This use of transition is not always so clear; there are those who choose to break the rules, as did Merce Cunningham in 1953. In his dance *Septet*, the dancers' entrances and exits at the end of each section use ordinary movements such as shaking hands and nods of goodbye. This odd technique draws attention to the gaps in between the sections, making the transitions as significant as the main dance.

Task 3

Compose two motifs which contain very different actions and qualities, eg

- fast jumps and swings
- gentle turns and gestures.

Experiment with them in the five ways listed below:

1. with a fast, abrupt link;
2. overlap them, ie start the second motif during the end of the first;
3. make a complicated phrase to link them;
4. use a segment of each of them to make the link;
5. find a smooth efficient way to link them.

Show each other your ideas and discuss which ones worked the best and why. Be ready for some surprises!

4. Highlights: certain moments of the dance will stand out as being most memorable. This can be achieved by playing with the quality, space or time; by adding, changing or contrasting and making movement stronger/weaker, longer/shorter, and so on. By placing highlights carefully you can express the intention of your dance more clearly to the audience.

In Paul Taylor's *Aureole* (1962) the delicate movement is highlighted by the unexpected, for example one dancer exits doing bouncy jumps then re-enters followed by another and returns again in a bouncy trio. This is a lovely example of building to a highlight. The final section of the dance is a more complicated version of itself. It exaggerates and decorates the original movement by distorting shapes which were previously straight or angular into zig-zags, turned-in or flexed. The tempo also crescendos to a headlong, seemingly frantic and out-of-control pace. Even the space is disturbed by emphasising the upstage left, downstage right diagonal which was not used in the earlier section. Taylor rushes the whole form into a crushing finale with great impact.

Task 4

In a solo use the following movements:

- running
- falling
- jumping
- stillness
- gentle arm gestures.

Create highlights:
- repeat one movement more times each time you do it;
- gradually decrease or increase the size of one of the movements each time you do it;
- suddenly interrupt one of the movements, for example the run with a stillness.

Show your solo to a partner and allow them to comment on whether or not these highlights hold their interest. Consider questions like:

Was there enough build up?
Were some highlights more important so that they became climaxes?

5. **Unity, Variety, Contrast**: these three elements work together in the forming process. The idea within the dance glues them together and when composing you should always keep this in mind. As you compose the movement be aware that it is appropriate to what you are expressing. Your dance idea and movements should develop logically and unite together. Naturally you will add variety in order to avoid being too monotonous and to give shading to the central image.

Contrast provides variety but it is a special type, introducing as it does new material. This could be a new point of view, a totally different quality or an obvious break from the central concern. Obvious use of contrast can be seen in the work of Michael Clark in his *I am Curious Orange*. A slow, lamentful balletic solo is followed immediately by the dancer tearing off her point shoes and performing a fast, energetic, frenetic dance.

Task 5

In groups of six, compose a short piece based on a basketball match called 'Time Out'. Using ideas such as the two teams, the ball, the referee, the tactics, the crowd, find movements which use action and reaction. As you work be aware of providing variety and contrast while retaining the unity of the idea.

6. Chance: the pioneers of chance as a device can be found in the music of John Cage and his partner, choreographer Merce Cunningham. Chance uses coincidence or fate to produce content and form perhaps by the throw of a dice, coins, anything. This determines the form which remains unchanged throughout the work. The dice may even be thrown during performance to decide which phrases of movement will be danced in which order – in this way the dance will be different each time it is performed. The task in Chapter 2 based on actions (p37) used this device.

Task 6

Find a short fairy story and cut it up into words, phrases or sentences. In a group of three or four, distribute the lines randomly and read the rearranged version. Each person takes a section of this and creates a brief dance from the words in any way they choose to abstract. (You may decide to read the words as accompaniment). Watch each other, then dance them in random order. You can create a group dance by learning each other's phrases and weaving in and out in any way you feel may work. Try to ensure that the group dance holds together in its transitions, highlights, unity, variety, contrast.

Structures for dance composition

These are set models that have been found to work well in the arts; classical frameworks which can be found in music, art and literature. They determine the overall structure of a dance but the movement material within this may be shaped by any of the previous devices. These structures are known as *sequential, contrapuntal, narrative* and *natural* structures, and they can be mixed.

Sequential structures

These have sections which follow each other in a definite order. Each section has a theme and is identified by a letter. A is the first, B the second and so on. The sections have unity by sharing something common to both sections.

1. AB Form

The simplest form, consisting of theme (A) and a contrasting or developed theme (B) linked by a transition called a *bridge*. Obviously this provides unity, variety, contrast and transition.

2. ABA Form

Again, this form gives order, consisting of a theme (A), developed theme (B) and return to the first theme (A). This gives a simple, well balanced structure.

3. ABACADA – Rondo Form

The A theme is first stated, then keeps returning in pure or varied form after related or contrasting themes are shown. A must be interesting enough to stand repetition. It is an easily enjoyable form because of its balance of repetition, variation and contrast. It is a typical form for many folk songs and dances, for example *Sergeant Early's Dream* by Christopher Bruce.

Task 7

Find a short piece of folk music, for example from Ireland or South America and listen to it. Divide it into sections – A, B, C etc. Compose a dance reflecting the simple structure of the music. Take care with the transitions between the sections and appropriate use of repetition, variation and contrast. It may help to use movements like simple steps, changes of direction and jumps.

Contrapuntal structures

Like the sequential ones, contrapuntal structures are found in music. These have a single theme which plays against itself, against one or more other themes or is woven through the entire length of the piece. Two or more strands are being heard or seen at the same time and so it can create a complex structure. The theme motif needs to be very clear and obvious to an audience so that the motif and how it is varied can be detected and appreciated throughout the piece. There are three principal contrapuntal structures:

1. **Bass ground** – A single theme is the opening statement which repeats through the whole piece while other themes play against its rhythmical pattern. In dance it is useful for themes which involve group opposition, inevitability, tenacity or a solo figure versus a group. It is challenging to dancers because of the rhythmic variety possible.

2. **Round or canon** – A round consists of a simple melody which is imitated and repeated against itself at different intervals. The melody is the same in all parts, whereas in a canon the original theme is often developed (see also Chapter 6 p90). 'London's Burning' is a good example of a round.

3. **Fugue** – This makes interesting dance even though it is complicated and irregular. The main theme interweaves with counter themes and as in motif development the melody (movement) can be inverted, reversed, shortened, slowed down, lengthened. The fugue usually builds to an exciting climax then quietens to a softer repetition of the opening. It can be valuable in developing dramatic ideas. Ian Spink used a fugue composed by Bach to transform a play into an abstract dance. Ordinary gestures such as picking up the telephone are repeated in strict rhythm and so become strange movements. The movements are developed like a fugue, each part eventually coming together to create something new. In this way Spink achieves his characteristic blend of text, dance, theatre and music.

Task 8

In groups of four, find motifs which use cooking actions (eg whisk, stir, chop). Make one motif four counts and describe only one cooking action, another for six counts using two cooking actions; the third for 12 counts and using as many cooking actions as possible. Adding other movement where appropriate to create exits and entrances, compose a dance called 'Mad Chefs'. Give the dance three sections; one is Bass ground; another a Round and the last a Fugue.

Narrative structure

Both modern dance and ballet use stories for content and structure. The plot can be made more exciting by the characters, locations, flashbacks, dreams and dance easily conveys fantasy, memory and nightmares. Short stories, autobiographies, your own diary, myths, fables all provide rich stimulus and a ready way of forming a dance. They can also exploit psychological effects as in Graham's *Errand into the Maze* (1947) where we see the heroine's journey into a maze and confrontation with the minotaur as told in the Greek legend. At the same time it signifies an exploration of her own fears and doubts.

Another example is Glen Tetley's *The Tempest* (1979) which goes beyond the Shakespearian tale by depicting events which are only hinted at in the text. In this way he uses the strengths of dance to create character.

Natural structures

The natural world can give structure and form to dance. Images such as day and night, seasons and life cycles (a butterfly or human) can easily stimulate improvisation and provide a structure.

An example of this is Paul Taylor's *Orbs* (1966). The six parts include Venusian Spring, Martian Summer, Terrestial Autumn and Plutonian Winter and the dancers are cast as planets and moons. Taylor symbolises the sun. He explores the cycle of the seasons and weaves in the feeling of the strength of natural forces over which humans have no control.

OVERALL FORM

Drawing together the ideas of this chapter it becomes clear that as you compose you must be aware of certain ingredients:

- clear movement phrasing;
- logical development of chosen image(s) and motifs;
- balance of repetition and variation;
- providing sufficient contrast.

With sufficient attention to these concerns the dance will begin to show a clear overall organisation and flow. This may determine whether the dance has a slow lyrical nature or moves along quickly and athletically. Some dances fall into contrasting sections so it is important to 'pace' the composition. A gradual preparation for the main highlight of the dance, the *climax*, is a part of the pacing process. An appropriate combination of the timing of the dance sequences, highlights and transitions will lead towards an inevitable ending for the dance. This may be a return to the opening, an end to the story, highly energised, a fade out or into stillness, but whatever you choose it must be decisive and evolve from the rest of the dance. Remember it will be the last thing that the audience will see so it must be worth watching. The overall form of the finished dance will meet the needs of the choreographer's ideas, the performers and the audience.

THE COMPOSITION PROCESS

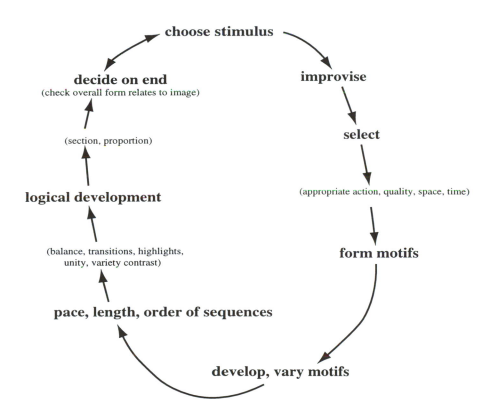

choose stimulus

decide on end
(check overall form relates to image)

improvise

(section, proportion)

select

logical development

(appropriate action, quality, space, time)

(balance, transitions, highlights,
unity, variety contrast)

form motifs

pace, length, order of sequences

develop, vary motifs

REFERENCES

Further Reading

Cohen, Selma Jane (1966) *The Modern Dance, Seven Statements of Belief*, Wesleyan University Press.

H'Doubler, Margaret N. (1974) *Dance: A Creative Art Experience*, University of Wisconsin Press.

Humphrey, Doris *The Art of Making Dances*, Grove Press.

Music

Task 2 – Mozart Concerto no 21 in C major for piano and orchestra, 2nd movement, *or* Bob Marley, 'Exodus', Island 9498.

Task 4 – Philip Glass, *Dance Pieces* CBS MK 39539.

Task 5 – David Byrne, *Songs from the Catherine Wheel*, Sire Records, SRK 3645.

Task 6 – *Le Mythe des Voix Bulgaires*, LC8259.

Task 7 – *Musique du Perou et de Bolivie*, Illique, Playa Sound KP9812.

Task 8 – Dance Technic track 1 side B available D W S Harry, Primrose Studios, Lancaster.

SIX ■ GROUP DANCE

MORE THAN A SOLO

So far we have considered dance composition mainly as the creation shaping and forming of movement from a chosen stimulus. One of the most enjoyable aspects of dance is dancing with others in a duet or group. However, when composing for more than one dancer additional issues need to be considered.

'Speaking beyond the movement for each individual dancer is the movement throughout the whole piece, and throughout all the parts that make the structure.'

Twyla Tharp[1]

PARTNER WORK

In a duet each dancer is essential to the whole. It is not a solo for two people but involves communication – simple visual design, touching, moving at the same time and in conversation with each other. There must be an involvement between the two which allows movement to be organised in a number of ways:

- leading and following;
- questioning and answering;
- meeting and parting;
- symmetry and asymmetry;
- matching and mirroring;
- contrast and complement;
- physical contact;
- co-operation and confrontation.

[1]Twyla Tharp, *The Dance Makers*, Elinor Rogosin, Walker and Co. 1980, pp. 138–9.

Robert Cohan's *Hunter of Angels* is a duet based on the relationship of the twins Jacob and Esau. It uses mirrored movement to emphasise their twin relationship. It also uses contact between the dancers to make an interesting struggle.

Task 1

In pairs:

1. Mirror each other with easy repeated movements and stillnesses, then make faster, more complicated phrases. Try to keep going as quickly and yet as accurately as possible. This will probably result in your varying on your partner's movement and can produce some interesting results.

2. One dancer is the clay and the other the sculptor. Mould the clay into many shapes. Develop this into impulses so that it becomes pushing/ pulling, the passive person following the other into swing, rise, fall, roll, etc. If you are the passive dancer try not to anticipate, let your partner do the moving for you.

Task 2

Look at the photograph of *The Strange Party* and notice the following groups left to right:

1. Three figures in masks, dress suit, glittery costume and cape.
2. Pierrot surrounded by three young girls.
3. Two masked females in fancy dress.

Consider this description: 'The whole scene had a mysterious air of festivity.' Create a piece which starts with the groupings in the photograph and develop entrances, exits, different groupings and so on.

SMALL GROUPS

Trios, quartets, quintets, sextets etc give rise to even more possibilities of arranging relationships between the dancers. For example in a trio combinations can be two versus one; all three together; one versus one

6.1 *THE STRANGE PARTY (1981) choreography Linda Rickett-Young*

versus one. Glen Tetley's *Pierrot Lunaire* is a classical story of the third party destroying a couple. In Robert Cohan's *Stabat Mater* Vivaldi's music is concerned with the sacred number three, and this is reflected in the use of a trio or trios in the dance.

Similarly you can explore the possibilities of groups of any size. Remember, however, that the number of dancers you choose must be appropriate.

All the devices and structures for dance composition from Chapter 4 are enriched when used for groups. You should consider the number and placement on the stage of the dancers when developing motifs or when using structures such as ABA. The more dancers using the same motif the more impact there will be. This could also provide a strong background for a solo dancer presenting a contrasting or complementary theme.

ORGANISING GROUP MOVEMENT IN SPACE

Once group shapes have been chosen you must decide where to put them on the stage. This, as previously mentioned in Chapter 2, can be a conventional design or a less formal arrangement which leaves the audience to select what to watch and when. The latter approach can lead to the use of less familiar venues such as parks and even roof tops!

Task 3

In a large group create and learn four short movement phrases. Organise two dances, one which uses clear group formations and the centre and diagonals, the other which scatters the dancers loosely around the stage. Watch the final result and discuss the differences.

Different types of groupings in space often go with certain styles. For instance one would expect to see more formal lines in classical ballet such as Fokine's *Les Sylphides* than in modern works like Richard Alston's *Wildlife*. In these two very different dances, the way that groups are organised in space also relates to the way that the set is designed.

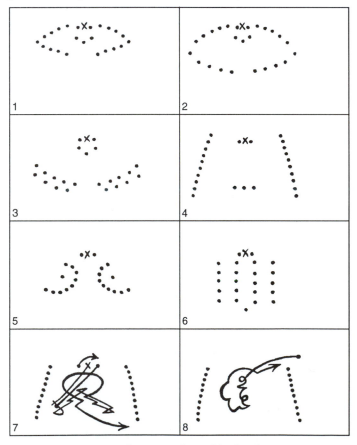

6.2 *LES SYLPHIDES (1909), choreography Mikhail Fokine*

6.3   WILDLIFE (1984) *choreography Richard Alston for Rambert Dance*

The set of *Sylphides* is realistic and static in contrast to the constantly changing mobiles in *Wildlife*. The stage is also divided in very different ways which would obviously affect the group shapes. Folk dance often uses simple lines and circles to give ideas of ritual, symbol and social exchange.

ORGANISING GROUP MOVEMENT IN TIME

One of the most satisfying ways of designing groups is to organise *when* dancers move. They may move all at the same time (in *unison*) or one after the other (in *canon*). Within these two structures there are many possibilities, leading to a rich variety of expression.

Unison

Dancers execute:

- the same movement at the same time;
- similar or complementary movement at the same time;
- contrasting movement at the same time.

Canon

This type of movement usually occurs in strict order as each dancer in turn performs an entire motif like an echo. Each dancer stops moving when the motif is finished. This very simple canon can be made more interesting by overlapping movement so that each dancer starts before

6.4   Helter-Skelter Youth Dance

6.5   THE MAD BAD LINE (1990) choreography Linda Rickett-Young

the one in front has finished. The dancers can also overlap motifs but finish at the same time, all doing the same thing.

Another canon structure involves a group dancing the same motif at the same time but from different starting points. So one dancer may carry out counts one to eight whereas another may start at count six, ie 67812345 and so on. This can give a complex, dense and visually interesting look.

Of course, all these canons can be developed and varied by using the same, similar or contrasting movement, and there is scope to add stillness, change level, direction, facing, stage placement, and to vary the quality and order of movements as well. Organising can be tricky. Persevere and experiment, because it will enrich your compositions.

6.6 ATOM SPLIT (1981) *choreography Linda Rickett-Young*

Task 4

From the photograph entitled *Atom Split*, create a dance which depicts what happens just before and when **THE BOMB** is dropped. There are two main groups of dancers, the scientists and 'the rest'. Give these groups contrasting motifs. Compose a dance which concentrates on using various types of unison and canon. Movements which may be useful are:

- a vibration of hands and whole body
- slow uninterrupted walking
- running with sudden falls.

Task 5

Watch a video of Twyla Tharp's *The Catherine Wheel* and note down as many examples of unison and canon as you can see. Compare notes with the rest of the group and try to explain how and why the timings succeeded.

6.7 *DANCESCAPES (1983) choreography Linda Rickett-Young for Tightrope Dance Company*

GROUP TRUST AND CONTACT

The interest of group shapes, placement and timings are emphasised by building trust between the dancers so that you can use contact. This is a special skill and a whole technique of dance has been created around it. It is called *Contact Improvisation* and was invented by American gymnast Steve Paxton, who later studied dance. Using his experience he produced a style based on giving and taking weight, on trusting someone to be there if you decide to fall or lean or bounce off them. In performance it is improvised and emphasises natural movement, taking risk and responsibility for each other. Paxton was part of a dance revolution in the States in the sixties which was based in Judson's

Church, from which the group took their name. Other famous dancers such as Trisha Brown and Douglas Dunn were involved. Like Paxton, they were a part of this post modern new dance style, many of whom had worked in the Merce Cunningham Dance Company before leaving to explore and develop their own styles.

Obviously this type of work requires practice like any other technique. Here are a few trust exercises that you may like to try and may give you confidence to use contact in your compositions.

Task 6

1. **The Circle of Trust:** One person stands in the centre of a circle of five or six others. With feet glued to the centre spot, that person keeps the body straight and tilts off-balance towards the circle. The others gently take the weight and push the person back to the centre. Increase the size of the fall as confidence increases. Everyone takes a turn to be in the middle.

2. **Park Bench**: In twos, sit on a bench with arms touching, looking straight ahead. Alternate sitting and standing, trying to keep together as much as possible.

3. **Joint Journey**: In twos, travel the length of the room without loss of contact. Try to vary the way you travel and the parts of the body which are in contact. Include such actions as sliding, spinning, rolling, carrying, jumping, falling (and being caught!), lowering and lifting etc.

It is well worth experimenting in duets and larger groups with simple hand holds and counterbalances. Feel exactly how much or little energy is necessary for counterbalancing with someone else before the moment when balance is lost. Similarly other contact situations such as lifting, lowering, catching and throwing, supporting or assisted jumps can have exciting results. Improvise with rolling around on the floor softly, finding moments of stillness that give support to a partner in interesting shapes. The possibilities are many and when a higher level of competence is reached flying through the air to be caught by a partner, as in the dances of company DV8, may be possible.

6.8   DEAD DREAMS OF MONOCHROME MEN (1988) *choreography Lloyd Newson for DV8*

94

Task 7

Below are a number of diagrams showing some duet support positions. Practice them singly trying to share the supportive positions. When confident arrange them in any order and link them with appropriate movement and transitions. At first slowly then try to add faster, more explosive dynamics.

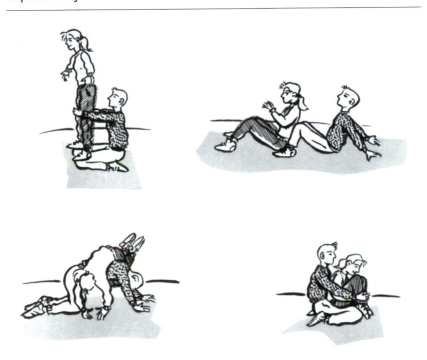

To help further at this stage, I will present a breakdown of the various ways in which dancers are used by Twyla Tharp in her dance *The Catherine Wheel*. The subject of the dance was St Catherine, the fourth century martyr who was persecuted for her efforts to be spiritually perfect in God's eyes. For a woman to be so forthright in those times would have been regarded suspiciously and not tolerated. As a result she was put on a spinning, burning spiked wheel (like our Catherine Wheel firework), but it exploded. She survived, but many pagans were killed in the blast. Later she was beheaded and subsequently martyred.

In the dance the main character, Sarah, tries like Catherine to attain perfection but she is haunted by this impossible ambition. She represents a future of extreme control in her attempt to imitate the perfect computerised image and therefore overcome her human failings. In contrast to Sarah there is a family: mother, father, son, daughter, maid, poet and the family pet. Their petty squabbles and small-minded greed represent impurity. Their movements are more everyday, walking, running, sitting, pushing and shoving. This contrasts with the smooth, more classical style of Sarah and her group. A third 'character' also features – a large pineapple which has strange, sinister powers to disrupt the family. It is sometimes a bribe; at other times an object of desire. Its very shadow is a weapon of destruction – a nuclear bomb or hand grenade. When cut into sections it resembles the Catherine Wheel itself.

So this is the setting into which the dancers are placed. There are many sections, each flowing easily into the next.

Prologue Section

A brief, fluid, graceful solo by Sarah, radiant in red, opens the dance. A sudden silhouette of the dark forces quickly follows. This effective contrast draws us into the illusion. A golden light (the pineapple) is passed from dancer to dancer, and as they see the light they remove their blindfolds. They are no longer shadows but real people, a real family. From silhouette into the light of their sitting-room they each dance in character. There are various short solos and duets as they mingle in an unfulfilling, frustrating fashion. In these three sub-sections the scene is set. The question in our minds is, which of these characters will succeed? The one in her solitude or the many? What are their destinies? By juxtaposing solo then group, a simple device, the question is clear. The music sings 'Run in a circle around their house.'

Section 2: Their Lives Revealed

We return to Sarah's solo, now joined by the perfect computer figure to make a duet. The electronic image calls and Sarah answers, attempting to perform the perfect adage to attain perfection. Suddenly we return to the silhouette of a duet dancing with the pineapple. Their plight is indolence and greed. Mother busks a dance on the street to earn money and tries to give the son and daughter a dancing lesson. They are hopeless, even when bribed by the pineapple. Father grabs the pineapple and uses it to bribe the pet and the maid. All this fast moving interaction between characters shows us the cacophony of unsatisfactory relationships and interference, revealed in the hectic way they cut haphazardly through the space – here, there, everywhere. It is enough to drive anyone mad.

By now Sarah is almost insane too. Crazed by her attempts to achieve perfection, her face contorts hideously, yet still she continues to follow the computer's lead. Her discipline is enforced by the entrance of a group of four blindfolded dancers. In highly organised unison and canon they perform their routines with strategic clarity and control. Sarah's resolve is strengthened. Four more dancers enter in the black and red uniform. Motifs are performed repeatedly with different facings in geometric floor pattern and military precision, blindfold – the blind leading the blind.

In this second section the journey begins for both groups. Their different personal qualities, lives and fates are unravelled before our eyes. A rabble of a family, desperate hopelessness and a woman certain of her destiny with an army to support her. Tharp has developed the relationships of the two groups not only by effective juxtaposition in time, but also in the differing ways that they use space and quality.

Section 3: The Fall, Martyrdom

The pineapple starts to become more noticeable. In the opening the silhouettes re-run the contentions between the various family members. They are selfish and materialistic. Mother takes the children busking. They are still hopeless! Enter the poet. Mother sees a way of lightening her responsibilities and introduces him to her daughter. The poet steals the pineapple. More and more dissatisfaction in the to and fro of the frantic motifs.

Meanwhile Sarah and her army are crumbling in despair and self-torture. She tried to resist and is tempted by the others. Their hand movements threaten and torture her. They are closer to her than before, imprisoned by bars which descend around them. At every turn her escape is blocked. It is too late, and as her ideals crumble around her the rubble and ruin leaves her only one path, martyrdom.

The family arguments continue. The poet is drawn in as mother lures him to taste the pineapple, like Eve with the apple. The poet, like Sarah, will fall. Images bounce rapidly from shadow to reality, from Sarah's tortured face to the maid's contorted facial expressions. Everyone, it seems, is on a path to self-destruction. The pineapple is devoured as the song states 'We just let things slide. All the way home. Over all these years. And nothing was done. And now the clock has stopped.'

It is too late. After the bomb has dropped, the entire contents of the home fly across the stage and the poles once again descend. Trapped! This longer section is interesting in the way that it reaches a climax through increasingly fast-paced switches between Sarah, the family and back again. This winds up the earlier, slower pace which emphasised the family's increased isolation from each other as they all blame each other and the band sings 'They fall through the cracks.' Sarah is more and more alone within her group.

Section 4: Clearing Up

The army in the black and red start to sweep up to clear the debris from the family home. It is piled into a net and hoisted high up above the stage. Mother and father dance a remorseful duet but it is too late and the family still show lack of direction in the continued swopping of partners in various duets.

Sarah and four of her army now with blindfolds removed, dance as solo versus group with, for the first time, contact. Cut to the family as shadows and reality still fall over themselves and each other. Sarah and her group come into closer contact. The family as shadows build a human pyramid to reach the remains of their home. The to-ing and fro-ing speeds up once again as the family and Sarah's ambitions are both obviously unreachable. The family's net of possessions is placed on Sarah's shoulders as her burden too. Here the almost cinematic cuts from one group to the other make clear the futility of both groups' ideals. The questions posed in the opening section are answered. Although Sarah and the family seem so different, neither will succeed. Destiny is the same for both, failure. All they can do is clear up some of each other's mess or carry the burden of the other. There is no answer and, like a one-way street, no turning back.

Section 5: The Epilogue

So what does Tharp offer us in our hopelessness? Sarah appears glorious in gold with her blindfolded army and they repeat the unison of section 2 around her as she turns and turns, travelling amongst them. But the movement quality is lighter, finer, more delicate; a clear variation of the motif. In unison and then canon they rise above their previous stations. This is a delicate transition into the real crashing climax of the final section.

Section 6: The Golden Section

Dancers in gold costumes burst onto the stage united by a positive energy. Tharp likens it to a realisation of pre-christian values, as the sun is recognised as a life-sustaining energy. The various characters come together to resolve the conflict, not through Catherine's academic discipline, nor through human potential. As all the dancers are pushed to their physical limits using a mega-mix of all the previous motifs with renewed vigour, Tharp's movement invention symbolises the positivity of her final conclusions.

In movement terms dancers criss-cross the stage in duets, unison, canon and overlapping canons through space. It is like a firework display as athletic explosive contact sparks everywhere. The music plays 'moving every direction'. Relaxed, 'laid back' solos are offset against large group canons as all the dancers come on stage together for the first time. This is followed by duets, trios, gradually building to a sextet. Then duet, solo, male quartet, and again duets, on and on at an impressively relentless pace, never-ending energy, everyone supported by it. A simple unison star jump by all brings everyone momentarily together, only to spark off into smaller groups again and then a short female solo which merges gradually into a male solo. As this ricochets the dance ends in mid-air. The energy still reverberates after the curtain has gone down, it leaves us breathless.

In this final section the movement pushes on effortlessly, naturally and enjoyably. The pagan Earth Goddess and the Fire God combine through the air with the flow of water to give us pure gold: the planet's true potential. It is a powerful unifying of all the dancers together that gives the climax and Tharp has given us much food for thought.

The dance blends section to section, solo, duet, trios, quartets and larger groups in a relationship which gradually reveals the story and leaves the brilliant finale to thrill us. A great deal of this is dependent on how the groupings and relationships between the dancers are organised. The timings on the sections below reveal an interesting direct brevity in Sarah's sections in comparison to the family dances. Sarah's motifs are more stylised 'dancey' movements, whereas the family's more natural vocabulary is more extended in style. Also there are more complicated relationships within the family than that of Sarah and her conscience.

SECTION TIMINGS OF *THE CATHERINE WHEEL*

SECTION 1. INTRODUCTION
Sarah's solo	1 min.	
Family section	7 mins.	= 8 mins. total

SECTION 2. THEIR LIVES REVEALED
Sarah solo/duet	1 min.	
Family relationships developed	4 mins.	
Sarah with group	4 mins.	= 9 mins. total

SECTION 3. THE FALL and MARTYRDOM
Family/poet	3 mins.	
Sarah with group	3 mins.	
Family/bomb drops	18 mins.	= 24 mins. total

SECTION 4. CLEARING-UP
Sarah's army/family	6 mins.	
Sarah	3 mins.	
Fast cuts from one to the other	3 mins.	= 12 mins. total

SECTION 5. EPILOGUE
Sarah with group	5 mins.

SECTION 6. THE GOLDEN SECTION
All dancers	14 mins.

TOTAL RUNNING TIME = 1 HOUR 12 MINUTES

So what can we conclude from these timings? The distinct family sections total 38 minutes in comparison to Sarah's 18 minutes, therefore the family sections represent nearly 50 per cent of the total running time whereas Sarah's are only about 25 per cent. The Golden Section is roughly 15 per cent, leaving 10 per cent for the sections which have a great deal of to-ing and fro-ing. This 10 per cent shows how, in time, the rapid shifts from one to the other make clear the similarities between Sarah and the family in spite of first impressions.

Tharp uses the groupings of the dancers to bring balance into the whole dance. The uniform, disciplined, direct qualities of Sarah and her army make hard-hitting fast statements and reflect her tunnel vision and their blindness. In contrast, the family have no real sense of direction alone or together. Their frantic, pointless lives and movements spend a great deal of time going nowhere. When the two contrasting groups merge they share the same fate and Tharp reveals her mastery of manœuvre as she keeps this brief and to the point. After much effective and dramatic build-up (41 minutes, more than 50 per cent of the total running time), their differences are of no consequence to their fates.

Finally the Golden Section is a fitting climax to the lyrics of David Byrne's song 'And they're enjoying themselves. Movin' in every direction with their eyes wide open.' The dancers bathe in the nourishing rays of the sun; a simple primeval energy which can save the planet if we allow it to. They dance together, all fifteen of them, as though they were one, in unison and canon, supporting each other in a complete sharing of all their varied strengths, weaknesses and characters. *The Catherine Wheel* is almost Shakespearian in its plot and character development.

DANCING IN GROUPS – A FINAL WORD

Sometimes you may be involved in a group making the dance with others and this can be satisfying and fun. When you dance in a piece there is a limit to what you see of its design and form, so you should also try to compose for other people without dancing in the composition.

At first this will feel difficult because it is a big responsibility, but try to be clear about what movements and images you are using. Listen to your dancers. Do they have a problem with a certain action or a transition? Sometimes the dancers' own movements can add to your ideas so try to be alert to how they move. Have you considered giving ideas for improvisation then choosing from what the dancers do? This could be a satisfying alternative to teaching chunks of movement to them. Your composition may even be based on the dancers' special features and differences.

As choreographer you will face many choices. Remember, if you have nothing worth throwing away, you probably have nothing worth keeping.

REFERENCES

Further Reading

Ellfeldt, Lois (1974) *A Primer for Choreographers*, Dance Books.
Morgenroth, Joyce (1987) *Dance Improvisation*, University of Pittsburgh Press.
Tuffnell and Crickmay (1990) *Body, Space, Image*, Virago Press.

Video

The Catherine Wheel, Twyla Tharp, Castle Hendring, 8 Northfield Prospect, Putney Bridge Road, London SW18 1PE.
Rushes, Siobahn Davies, National Resource Centre for Dance, University of Surrey, Guildford, Surrey GU2 5XH.
The Hunter of Angels, Robert Cohan. Available from the National Resource Centre for Dance (as above).

Music

Task 2 – *Prospero's Books*, Michael Nyman, Decca 425 224-4.
Task 3 – Dance Technics, side A, track 2.
Task 4 – *Kraftwerk*, Vertigo 6641 077.
Task 7 – Soundtrack from 'The Big Blue' by Eric Serra.

SEVEN ■ ACCOMPANIMENT FOR DANCE

When choosing what to use to accompany your dance it is tempting to choose your favourite band or singer, but often what you should ask is whether you need any sound at all. Ideally a composer would offer to write a score for you, note for note to match your dance, but if you are at school willing composers are probably a bit thin on the ground! That is why this chapter may help you to become aware of the many alternatives to that much heard statement, 'I cannot find any music.'

SOUND

Natural Sounds and Sounds from your Environment

These could be the sounds of a storm, a railway station, washing machine, birds, whale sounds, a football crowd. When used carefully these can create great atmosphere. They can be mixed together with the sounds of musical instruments. Robert Cohan's *Forest* is danced to a score comprising wind in the trees, insects, birds, rain and thunder and was written after the choreography was completed. In an impressionistic style there is no story, but the atmosphere of the forest is created. The dance motifs reveal scenes of the echoing calls of the forest creatures as they appear fleetingly among the undergrowth and treetops. The dance is similar to Cohan's *Nympheas* in that it explores the kaleidoscope images of the natural world.

Task 1

Take recordings outside in a busy street. Include sounds like footsteps, traffic, shops, trains etc. In a group of five or six devise a dance called 'Rush Hour'. Consider such ideas as a bus queue, fast walking patterns, supermarket shopping etc.

Vocal Sounds

A dance which uses live spoken accompaniment can emphasise and accent the images or the rhythms. The words may take a number of forms: melodic, song-like, disjointed, 'pure' sounds, breath, nonsense, in a different language.

Task 2

Choose one of Edward Lear's nonsense rhymes, a nursery rhyme or a poem by Lewis Carroll. Consider how you could develop its ideas to give movement phrases. Develop its rhythm, its images or its sounds for accompaniment. Make a trio from your movements. Below is an example of such a poem.

Extract from *Alice's Adventures in Wonderland* by Lewis Carroll:

. . . said Alice 'What sort of dance is it?'

'Why,' said the Gryphon, 'you first form into a line along the seashore – '

'Two lines!' cried the Mock Turtle. 'Seals, turtles, salmon, and so on: then when you've cleared all the jelly-fish out of the way – '

. . . ' – you advance twice – '

'Each with a lobster as a partner!' cried the Gryphon.

'Of course,' the Mock Turtle said: 'advance twice, set to partners – '

' – change lobsters, and retire in same order,' continued the Gryphon.

'Then you know,' the Mock Turtle went on, 'you throw the – '

'The lobsters!' shouted the Gryphon, with a bound in the air.

' – as far out to sea as you can – '

'Swim after them!' screamed the Gryphon.

'Turn a somersault in the sea!' screamed the Gryphon.

'Turn a somersault in the sea!' cried the Mock Turtle, capering wildly about.

'Change lobsters again!' yelled the Gryphon at the top of its voice.

'Back to land again, and – that's all the first figure,' said the Mock Turtle, suddenly dropping his voice; and the two creatures, who had been jumping around like mad things all this time, sat down again sadly and quietly, and looked at Alice . . .

> So they began solemnly dancing round and round Alice, every now and then treading on her toes when they passed too close, and waving their fore-paws to mark the time . . .

The rich images of movement in the above passage are many and the build up into the energetic, frantic dynamics of the duo before starting their solemn dance could be great fun to use. The words they use could also be useful.

In Richard Alston's *Rainbow Bandit* a sound collage of much repeated word phrases is gradually abbreviated and looped so that it becomes intensely rhythmic, and the motifs respond to this. Poetry and stories can be the dance stimulus as well as accompaniment, by the dancers, a narrator or on tape.

Gary Lambert of Rambert Dance Company choreographed a dance entitled *Longevity*. The duet was dedicated to North American civil rights leader Martin Luther King who was assassinated on 4 April 1968. The dance uses a recording of a famous speech of his. The movement follows the rhythm of the words but it also uses the sense of some of the words in the motifs.

Task 3

Use the words of the poem below to make a sound collage which has a clear rhythmical feel.

We have come home
The gurglin' drums
Echo the stars
The forest howls
And between the trees
The dark sun appears.

By repeating certain words many times and adding pauses you can create driving rhythms like a rap which you may record as accompaniment or speak live during the dance. Try to make the final piece a loop, ending where it begins. The sounds and rhythms of the words will be most important in finding movement, but sometimes you may use the meaning of the words too.

Movement Sounds

Stamping feet, clapping hands, clicking fingers, softly rubbing palms together. In tap dance and Flamenco the rhythm of the feet are a crucial part of the whole dance form. In Flamenco the hands are also used with the help of the castanets to accent and reinforce the rhythms.

Task 4

Create a solo dance in which the only accompaniment is from your body, (a mix of breath, your voice, your hands, feet etc). Be aware of any rhythms you may create and the overall form of the dance.

SILENCE

The rhythm of the dance can be kept only in the body and so all the content, form and style relies solely on the movement. All kinds of movement can be successful: comic or serious, complex or simple, powerful or gentle. Sometimes a dance may have started with a piece of music as accompaniment but will actually benefit from being performed without it, or to another piece of music entirely.

Silence may be chosen for certain sections of a dance, or at the start or end. In Martha Graham's *Primitive Mysteries* the main dramatic rituals occur in the silent sections and this intensifies their power.

Mary Wigman in her Expressionistic style composed many of her early works in silence in the early 1900s. She pioneered a new dance form called 'Absolute Dance' and her works ranged from the gentle to the dark and sinister. Her style was strongly emotional, no doubt influenced by Isadora Duncan. In 1914 her *Witch Dance* used strange body shapes and clawing hands to express evil and mystery.

Task 5

In a group of five, compose together a dance in silence called 'Echoes'. Be aware of the different sorts of canons that you may find. Be alert to how you design the movement in space with regard to direction, level, facings, exits and entrances.

MUSIC

A piece of music may well inspire you to leap to your feet in the privacy of your bedroom. The trap that you may fall into is that of allowing the music to dominate the movement. Music provides a pulse, a driving force and it can be a strong stimulus as in the work of George Balanchine and Robert North, who both use their musicality as the mainspring of their work. They both work to make the final dance a complete blend of movement and music. Balanchine's *Agon* follows and is supported by the steady pulse of Stravinsky's music, but the dancers play around in a jazzy way with time and rhythm in the same way as the instruments of the orchestra. Balanchine and Stravinsky once described their work together as being for those who are able to *hear* the dance and *see* the music. To them, sound and movement were one and the same thing.

When composing a dance the relationship with the music can arise in several ways:

- dance and music composed simultaneously;
- dance created first and music created for it later;
- composed music with dance choreographed to it;
- dance and music created separately and performed for the first time together in performance (as seen in the work of Cunningham and Cage);
- a piece of suitable music is found for the dance while it is still in sketch form. In this way the dance may be shaped to suit the musical structure without the music totally dominating the movement.

Check list when choosing music

1. *Beware the Top Ten, old favourites and famous classics.* Often the lyrics or people's own strong feelings and connections are obstacles which may cloud the ideas which you are trying to express.
2. *Don't chop it or cut it!* It is inartistic to cut and rearrange someone else's music – it is also illegal. How would you like someone to rearrange your dance, or decide that they didn't need the middle bit and so throw it away?
3. *Quality.* Try to choose music which will not be scratched or sound as if it is being played underwater.

4. *Suitable balance*. A solo to a full symphony orchestra will not be easy. Consider the texture of the sound so that it is appropriate to the number of dancers and choice of images.

5. *Copyright*. There are laws which cover the use of music for performance; consider whether they might apply to you.

6. *Style*. Use the atmosphere of the music – Scottish ballad; Indian sitar; Renaissance, Impressionist or Neo-classical dance. If you choose to ignore it you must be able to explain why and how you are working against it.

7. *Using Pre-recorded music*. Take time to analyse its structure, tempo, metre, arrangement and instrumentation. Improvise to it and only when the music is clear to you can you be sure that it will not dictate the dance.

8. *In an ideal world* we would all dance to live music. Do you know a young musician or singer who may be interested in a bit of collaboration?

Task 6

In pairs create a 12 count phrase of movement and take turns in performing it to the following accompaniments:

- silence
- a piece of electronic music
- percussion instruments
- opera
- Irish music
- Radio 4

As you move speak the words which describe what you are doing, eg the counts, the actions, the quality etc.

Discuss the final results. How did the various accompaniments affect the movement?

The way you choose and work with accompaniment for your dances can help to make them more successful if you do not limit your choice to only one or two types of music or sound. Try to experiment by mixing, say, silence with music, or any of the different sorts of accompaniment together. Often music which makes good bathtime singing is best kept for the bubbles!

It is a good idea to listen properly to the music first and try to understand its tempo, metre etc. Make sure you are able to count it in a way which helps you to move with it. This may not be the way that the musician would count it, but it *will* help you to use the structure of the music in an imaginative way so that the dance is enhanced rather than restricted.

An interesting way of using metred music is to count it in different measures from that in which it is played. For example:

Music: 4-4-4-4-4-4   = 24 (4x6)
Dance: 7 – 9 – 8   = 24 (7+9+8)

This kind of imaginative counting makes the use of chart music more possible, because you are not allowing the rigid beat to limit your movement. The music of Igor Stravinsky caused problems in terms of counting when Vaslav Nijinsky chorographed *Le Sacré du Printemps* in 1913. Stravinsky was experimenting in a revolutionary way with rhythm to produce a new style of music. This was rather like the explorations of the painter Picasso who at the time found inspiration in the long-forgotten forms of African sculpture. Stravinsky made new use of strong accents and complex *polyrhythms* (as heard in African music). In the dance, too, Nijinsky shocked the ballet world, using heaviness and aggression and by using turn-in of the legs rather than the usual elegant light turn-out. In one section of *Le Sacré du Printemps* the young people of a pagan Russian community stamp out the offbeat accents of the music. The asymmetry and counterpoint of group movement on top of the steady 4/4 metre express the raw energy of pagan ritual.

Task 7

Choose a piece of music that is short and has a simple clear structure. Make sure you understand the structure. Choose a piece of country and western music, a gospel song or from the Blues. Some classical works, for example by Bach or Handel, may also be useful. Write down or draw the music in your own way and then put your own movement ideas alongside. For example, an opening melody in the music may make you think of large curving runs, fast jumps or collapses, whereas the next section may be more suited to long stillnesses and sustained isolated gestures.

Paying attention to the appropriate use of motif repetition, development and variation, to contrast, transition and climax make the score into a complete dance.

Counting, rhythm and structure are important when listening and choosing music for dance, but texture, tone and melody also need attention. In the early 20th century musicians like Ravel and artists like Paul Klee were experimenting with new ideas of expressive uses of colour. In painting it is easy to understand how colour could be fascinating, but in music? As Stravinsky experimented with rhythm Ravel was using musical tone colour in which we hear frogs croak and insects hum above the melody and rhythms, adding expression to the music. In *The Firebird*, by Stravinsky, the texture and tone of the music build to make a grand fanfare-like ending as Ivan and his princess are finally married. Fokine choreographed this in 1910, basing the dance on the Russian fairy tale and Stravinsky's music.

Below are extracts from a Russian fairy tale called *The Wizard of Kiev*. The greedy Tartars threatened Russia and in his fifteenth year Volg Vseslavich challenged them with an army of only 7000. This is how he did it.

His mother was a princess but it was said his father was a serpent; from the mother came his courage and from the father his skill and guile. At night he assumed the shape of a lion and hunted forest animals. When he fished he took the form of a pike. But by day he was a warrior and a leader of warriors.

An invasion threatened the land so he ventured to spy on the enemy's mountain stronghold. He turned into a ram and sped away with a flash of his guilded horns. For long days and nights through the wind and rains the ram travelled and at last halted on a mountain crag and watched.

One hour later a scarlet-crested bird lighted at the window of a chamber high in the fortress. It cocked its head to catch the words of the man and the woman within. The bird heard the Tartar Khan tell his wife how he would divide the rich lands between his sons. The woman cried, 'I dreamed two birds battled. A small northern bird slew a raven from the south. Do not raise your arm against him.'

But the Tartar cursed her dreaming. The listener at the window took wing. That night a destroyer struck the fortress. A ferret darted about the armory, tearing bowstrings and snapping arrows with its teeth.

Volg Vseslavich gathered his men and marched them to the Tartar fortress. No-one saw them come; not a footfall was heard. A sharp-eyed sentry scanning the walls might have seen ants in their thousands creeping in a single silent column underneath the iron gates. Within the strong-walled fortress the warriors sprang up where the tiny ants had been. Soldiers drew their swords against an invisible enemy. Someone saw a shadow of a wolf on the wall, then someone heard the beating wings of a falcon flying towards Russia. Left weaponless the Tartars were beaten.[1]

Task 8

Using appropriate music (see end of chapter) tell the story using characters, images and groups. You may choose to develop some sections, eg a celebration dance at the end and miss out others to make the story easier to understand. For this task it may be helpful to have an outside choreographer. You could use sounds and words with the music if you like.

Siobahn Davies' dance *Carnival* set to *Carnival of the Animals*, by Saint-Saens is such a piece. It uses the music framework clearly but not slavishly. It avoids limitation, for example by the way that Davies interprets the cuckoo as a lovelorn, hopeless suitor. The main motif is a simple arm gesture to show a sad heart beating as his beloved remains cool and aloof. The effect is witty and captivating. The golf-playing elephant uses 3/4 metre to swing clubs and trunk whilst falling and travelling with triplets. Another solo is of a lone swan gliding across the stage. The exquisite lines of the swan's wings and beak are at one with the smooth cello accompaniment.

[1]From the *Enchanted World; Wizards and Witches*, ed. B. Lehane, Time Life Books 1984.

Such solos and duets are interspersed with large group sections which bring the music to life with sensitive, often complex choreography. Groups of fishes and birds dive, flash and flutter before our eyes. The dancers are themselves both human and animal, at the same time weaving in and out of the musical structure. The music's sections, crescendos, accents and tempos are used by Davies with a intuitive sense of choice of movement and characterisation. It is fascinating, touching and fun.

Musical motifs

Like in the motifs used in dance composition, music uses *motifs which are simple melodic ideas*, repeated, developed, varied or contrasted. Examples in music of building from a motif include the following:

- change of metre from 4/4 to 7/8;
- transpose, ie up or down in scale;
- develop one part of the motif;
- play it backwards (*retrograde*);
- play in longer notes (*augmentation*);
- play a chord which uses all the notes of the original motif.

These should remind you of the previous list in Chapter 4 of dance motif development.

Task 9

Listen to Dave Brubeck's *Unsquare Dance*. It is in 7/8 metre which acts as the unifier. The variation of interwoven accents makes it highly regarded as a 20th century jazz classic. Study the diagram below to see if you can find a motif which is appropriate to the patterns of the bass notes and hand claps.

UNSQUARE DANCE METRE

Low instrument/bass

Claps

In the classical world Michel Fokine's *Les Sylphides* (1908), a one act ballet set to romantic piano music by Chopin, shows a clear and formal structure moving along close to the music. Although the music is mostly in dance forms such as the waltz and mazurka, other aspects of it made the choreography difficult. It has changes of mood, tempo and inconsistencies in the rhythms which Fokine used to create the pure romantic feel of floating above the music. Isadora Duncan, the first to use Chopin's music, is acknowledged as an influence on Fokine. She was the first to use extended movement phrases and less regular timings which work well with the ebb and flow of this music. The overall structure of the dance is a series of solos, duets and *corps de ballet* which changes with sections of the music.

These days there is an endless variety of music and sound available in record shops. But if the budget is small why not try to make your own?

7.1   FEET FIRST, *choreography Linda Rickett-Young*

REFERENCES

Further Reading

Music by Silver, Burdett and Ginn.
The Annotated Alice (1970), Lewis Carroll, Penguin Books.

Music

Task 6 – Bach, *Little Fugue in G minor.*
Handel, *Trio Sonata in A major Op. 5.*
Nanci Griffith, *Late Night Grand Hotel*, MCA10306.
Billie Holliday, *The Blues are Brewin'*, 16 classic tracks, MCA1688.
Task 8 – extracts from the following:
Les Mythes des Voix Bulgaires.
Folk Music of Bulgaria, Topic 12T107.
Folk Music of Turkey, Topic 12TS333.

EIGHT ■ EXTRAS AND ESSENTIALS

PROPS, MASKS, COSTUMES AND SET

When choosing these bear in mind that they must be a *necessary* part of the dance. If they are not actually the stimulus, they should emphasise the images, illusions and design.

'I used masks and props – the masks to have the dancer become something else; the props to extend the physical size in space (as extra bones and flesh).'

Alwin Nikolais[1]

Some examples of the use of props and costume in dance are:

- *Imago* where Alwin Nikolais clothes his dancers in strange arm extensions that look like extra bones, and in his *Masks, Props and Mobiles* a group of stretchy bags come to life and the surprise is to find that the sacks are an extension of the dancer inside.
- *The Green Table*, by Kurt Jooss, where a green baize snooker table represents the immovable political differences and games that explode around it. It also gives opportunity for rich development of level in the power struggle.
- *Ghost Dances* by Christopher Bruce. Here the death masks of the oppressors combined with the body painting emphasise their primitive, sinewy movement and their sinister presence.

Props

These can easily inspire dance because there are so many ways in which they can cause movement to happen. In the magical world of theatre a newspaper can be anything you wish it to be. You can pick it up to sweep the floor, cloak someone in it, roll it up and look through it, sit on it, stand on it. It can be smooth, spiky. You could even read it!

[1]Alwin Nikolais, *Vision of Modern Dance*, p114.

*8.1 IN A BAD WAY (1988) choreography by Linda Rickett-Young for BAD
Dance Company*

It may be the colour or feel or shape of the prop that gives you ideas
for movement. Sometimes it may be how the object itself moves – the
roll of an egg, the unfolding of a plastic bag. The property itself may
take on a meaning or meanings in dramatic situations, for example a
net tutu may become the leaves of a tree or a tennis racquet become
prison bars.

8.2 BAD LUCK, BAD TIMING (1988) choreography by Linda Rickett-Young for BAD Dance Company

The following is a suggested list of properties which you may wish to try:

chairs	rope	boxes	walking stick
elastic	feathers	bucket	paper bags
hoop	ladder	ballons	scarves
fabric	umbrella	broom	traffic cones
plastic flowers		lampshades	frying pan

117

Task 1

Collect a number of unrelated objects and then choose one of the Shakespeare plays, eg *A Midsummer Night's Dream*. Try to identify the main characters and the general plot (not too much detail). In *A Midsummer Night's Dream* there are some strong characters such as Oberon, Titania (King and Queen of the fairies), Puck, the lovers, Bottom and the fairy chorus. There is a general feeling of magic and mischief! Use the props with the characters to rewrite a short version of the story.

Masks

Masks have had a powerful influence on ritual dance and theatre since primitive times. They have been made of many different materials: wood, stone, metal, fibre, bone, clay, cloth, plants, feathers and many more. Whatever materials are easily to hand will be used to weave the magic spell and make the mask special in style to suit the ritual.

In many parts of the world the ritual dance has strong symbolic powers. For instance in Bali the *barong* is a monster who fights an evil monster, therefore exorcising evil from the community and warding off bad luck or illness. The *barong* consists of two dancers underneath a fantastic costume and mask.

Often the wearer of the mask is regarded as sacred or supernatural and the mask becomes holy, to be touched only by the special few. The mask gives the wearer a new identity, a god of nature or a spirit, often releasing inhibitions. In Mali, Africa a ritual mask dance is used to honour the death of their village dignitaries. Up to a week long the ritual establishes order and balance, pacifying the spirit of the dead. The masks can be up to sixteen feet high and are blade shaped. The dancers sweep the ground with the top of the mask in the ceremony, symbolically cleansing the ground.

Involving masks can be a challenging way of making dances. Masks can be made out of a simple brown paper-bag design, full and half head, nose and eyes only. They can be extremely intricately decorated with beads, sequins, plants, fabric or a simple copy of your own face in a clear mood. The list of characters and moods is endless.

Task 2

Using the signs of the Zodiac, create masks for the various symbols of the people in your group. Improvise around the personal characteristics of the signs, eg Capricorn is patient. Choreograph a dance that explores how they may react to each other.

Costumes

As with masks, what a dancer wears, whether simple black or lavish *Kathakali* costume, is to be regarded as an extension of the body. The simplest costume can be effective if appropriate to the range and mood of the movement. For instance, a lyrical style dance may well be best suited to light chiffon or silk. (See illustration *Five Brahms Waltzes in the Manner of Isadora Duncan*).

Of course dancing in pillowcases, hats, towels or wellington boots will suggest a more comic style, although sometimes, as in African dance, wellington boots can become the sound accompaniment by slapping and stamping. Merce Cunningham created a dance based around an oversize sweater which had no hole for the head but four sleeves! In *Free Fall Fashion* the silk of the costumes also served as props – scarves and flags (see illustrations).

Paul Taylor's *Three Epitaphs*, first choreographed in 1956 and more recently performed by the London Contemporary Dance Theatre shows three shapeless, almost two-dimensional human type creatures. Their slumping, crouching, spineless movement is enhanced by a simple costume, a black body-hugging cover-all with tiny mirrors on the hands designed by Robert Rauschenberg. The overall effect is both witty and sad.

The more elaborate costumes of the ugly sisters in Frederick Ashton's *Cinderella* establish the larger than life caricatures of the fairytale panto dames.

The many well-known choreographers throughout history have used costume designs which extend and strengthen the dance idea. Whether it be the illusion of traditional tutu of the classical dancer hovering lightly above the floor or the throw-away look of the post modern dancers as they perform on roof-tops, their costume helps us to know more about the style or the significance of a dance.

8.3 *FIVE BRAHMS WALTZES IN THE MANNER OF ISADORA DUNCAN (1976)*
choreography Frederick Ashton for Ballet Rambert

Set

From the 15th century onwards the beginnings of ballet as court entertainment always used the finest artists to design the scenery. Italy, France and England produced huge, splendid backdrops of realistic proportion and perspective.

In the 19th century the Romantic movement had a more natural look such as you might see in Ciceri's *Giselle*, choreography by Jean Coralli and Jules Perrot (1841). Later when Romantic Ballet developed, larger spectacles laid the foundation of a new approach to stage design.

Serge Diaghilef, an entrepreneur deeply committed to the work of visual artists such as Benois and Bakst, became interested in ballet and founded the Ballets Russes. He insisted on designer and choreographer working closely together. Benois designed for *Les Sylphides* and *Petrushka* and Bakst for *The Firebird* and *L'Après Midi d'un Faune*.

It was in the 20th century, in 1934, when Martha Graham with her less narrative style needing less realistic set and costume, worked with Japanese designer Isamu Noguchi. This collaboration changed the look of stage design. His sparse, free-standing sculpture-like sets were integral to the dance. For example in *Frontier* (1935), Noguchi's first work for Graham, the solo is set on a section of fence. Two ropes fly away

8.4 *FREE FALL FASHION (1984) choreography Linda Rickett-Young*

8.5 and 8.6 FREE FALL FASHION *(1984) choreography Linda Rickett-Young*

diagonally upwards from each side of the fence. The dance of this lone female pioneer is set in the vast space of American frontier lands. The dance reaches out in all directions from the territory of the fence, as does the set. Noguchi's design supports the emotional meaning of the dance, and the landscape in which the woman dances.

Later Merce Cunningham saw design as a completely different element. He saw dance, music and set as separate on stage and therefore broke the conventions of centuries. He collaborated with artists like Andy Warhol, Robert Rauschenberg and Jasper Johns. In *Rainforest* (1968) the dancers moved with, around and in spite of Warhol's helium-filled silver pillows.

Tables, chairs, curtains, ladders, boxes, ropes, bicycles, mobiles, scaffold, rubber-plants, planks of wood, all these give a richness of level and dimension to the dance. In a recent show, *Dinner-Dance*, (1991) by The Kosh, a complete kitchen was constructed on stage. Dancers disappear underneath the sink and into the fridge. They also fall from a great height off the table to be caught at the last minute by the passers-by. An atmosphere of domestic disagreements is created.

Richard Alston's *Wildlife* (1984) uses huge mobiles designed by Richard Smith. The dancers move around, under and through them, always echoing the sharp edges of the set, which itself moves by the use of electric motors. It turns and flies up and down. The music too, by Nigel Osborne, is influenced by the set until finally all the elements come together in a flat, zig-zag energy.

A final example of set design can be seen in the work of Pina Bausch. Dancers move on floors covered with dead leaves (*Bluebeard*, 1977) or mud (*Le Sacré du Printemps*, 1975), or ankle deep in pink and white flowers (*Carnations*, 1975). Her works of despair and terror are shocking and real. Dancers hurl themselves towards each other over and over again in hostile, surreal surroundings.

Task 3

Build a structure from any objects available. As a group, discuss what kind of place this might be: a city street, another planet, a house etc. Find suitable characters to inhabit the set and appropriate costumes and props for them. Improvise together, emphasising the imaginative use of the various objects.

Props, masks, set and costume should grow from the needs of the dance, not be added extras. It is a good idea to keep an eye out in charity shops for any interesting items that may be useful one day.

THE RULES AND YOU

This book may seem to be full of rules, facts, do's and don'ts, but what matters most is *how you use them*. Try to let them stimulate, not restrict, you. When you understand them you can break them as much as you like as long as you can explain why and how. They are there to be used to your advantage.

You may feel that you have nothing worth using for choreography, but allow yourself to follow up any vague whim or fancy and as you work the germ of an idea may start to take shape, even if it was not the idea you started with.

There are certain attitudes which you can cultivate which will help you to learn how to work. Try to be curious, involved, original, sensitive, resistant to clichés, adventurous, economical and self-critical in your work. When I am working with dance students I often see them in a process of learning how to work. It is fun and full of surprises, not the least of which are the discoveries that you may make about yourself. As you dance and compose ask yourself 'Why am I doing this dance?' and 'What am I trying to say?' Try to be clear about the images you are using, whether the concern is for a certain emotion, or movement or whatever. There are no rules about your choice of stimulus; indeed the main characteristic of modern dance is that it recognises the choreographer's concern as the main priority. There are as many possible dances as there are choreographers.

> **'Whatever one dances one is,'**
> *Martha Graham*[2]

In such a way in the 1970s the X6 Dance Collective explored dance and movement ideas which lay outside the traditional styles, much in the same way that the Judson group had done in the States in the sixties. This led to a new style of British modern dance which explored approaches such as release, contact improvisation, t'ai chi and political

[2]Martha Graham, *Dancemakers*, p25

concerns. Its influence was clearly demonstrated in such companies as the Extemporary Dance Theatre which originally worked with a blend of Graham-style contemporary and ballet but changed its emphasis to new dance with the appointment of Emlyn Claid, one of the original members of X6, as director in 1981. From Extemporary, dancers such as Lloyd Newson have founded their own companies. Newson's DV8 reacted against the lack of political concern in dance, but also took some ideas like contact improvisation much further to create a new style called *physical theatre.*

WHERE DO I GO FROM HERE?

The stimulus is chosen – all you can now do is work to compose a clear, simple, subtle presentation of it. This is a tough challenge, but hopefully the enjoyment of trying will encourage you to carry on. The excitement of taking risks, of trying to hold a balance between adding and throwing away and of making mistakes work for you are just a few of the strands in the tangled webs which you will weave. So what is left in this 'religion of the foot', as Isadora Duncan named it? The answer is that magic moment of a live dance performance. When composing you should have been continually preparing your dancers for this. As a dancer the technical and expressive aspects of the dance should have become a part of you so that your performance is a total involvement and projection of its overall form. You and the dance are one and the same thing.

As for the audience, they will make up their own minds. The same dance will be different for different people. In your dance the main intention or image will be surrounded by other hidden ones and often these are discovered by the audience and revealed to you later. What the audience perceives will obviously be influenced by who and what they are. You have no control over this. Indeed, I have had many such revelations from my audiences and often they have been absolutely correct, showing me something in a dance that I had overlooked. The audience's input is essential to the life of a dance.

It is worth considering here that there is no substitute for going to see live dance theatre. No doubt you will use video to study but it is nothing like the real thing. So, if and when you have a chance to go to see something, be there! It may not always be to your taste but that doesn't matter; seeing live dance will add to your growth of understanding, your resources on which to draw, and will promote the discovery of yourself in dance.

Whether as dancer, choreographer or audience the final prompt of this book is

'What does it mean to *you*?'

REFERENCES

Video

Interviews with Siobahn Davies, Ian Spink and Lloyd Newson. Digital Dance Lecture No 2 available from the National Resource Centre for Dance.

Music

Tasks 1,2,3, – Any Balinese, Indian or Thai music which can help set a mood, flow and drama.
'Ravel' by Tomita, RCA RK13412.
'Mussgorsky' by Tomita, RCA ARL 1-0838.
'World Service' by Man Jumping, EGED 49.
'Zoolook', Jean-Michel Jarre, Polydor POLH 15.
'Ancient Voices of Children' by George Crumb, Nonesuch H71255.

As we saw in Chapter 1, there are many forms of theatre dance in Britain today. Classical ballet, Contemporary dance, New Dance, African, Indian, Flamenco are some of the more obvious ones but by no means the only ones either in terms of performance and certainly not when we turn our attention to the many dance and movement styles in which people participate. This chapter will divide these many styles into the following sections:

1. Other styles of dance for performance.
2. Social dance.
3. The fitness factor.
4. Training.

DIFFERENT STYLES OF DANCE FOR PERFORMANCE

West End shows like *Cats, Starlight Express* and so on are the real commercial end of the dance spectrum. A very well-known example of such work is the musical *Chorusline* where the jazz dance style powerfully hits the beat. Jazz dance styles such as those of Matt Mattox and Bob Fosse are highly suited to the glitter and glamour of the commercial theatre.

The history of jazz dance is rooted in African rhythms brought to the USA with the slave trade in the early 1800s. In the deep south of the United States black slaves created jazz music and the movements to go with it. Movements consisted of a great deal of twisting and wiggling of the hips in a spontaneous fashion and continued to develop with the music into a mix of European and African styles.

Later it developed into crazes of such social dances as tango, rumba, samba and of course the charleston. The African legacy of hip gyration, low bent stance, rippling spine and limbs reacting to the beat of the drums was here to stay.

A style of show dance was born as a way for poor black people of America to make a little money, whether on street corners or in the shows (as depicted in the film *The Cotton Club*). Tap dance was and still is a popular entertaining style. Dancers like Katherine Dunham and Pearl Primus researched African and Carribean dances and adapted them into jazz and contemporary styles for stage. Gradually jazz became a recognised system of technical training, differing with the style of the teacher and known for its physically demanding exercises.

American tap dance blended African styles with the European clog dances and Irish jigs, reels and step dancing. Fred Astaire showed clearly the European tap style, an upright carriage of the torso combined with a smoother, less bouncy look than the American style. Another 'great', Gene Kelly, blended jazz style with a more black influenced tap. The stage musical *42nd Street* is typical of the white American style. It is interesting to note here that much black talent would never have become known because of the racism of those times, if it were not for such shows. An old film, *Stormy Weather*, is well worth searching out to see the high quality of dancing from the all-black cast.

In Britain these styles of jazz and tap dance now form a backbone of stage shows. The musical *Stepping Out* by Richard Harris has done much to popularise tap since the decline of Hollywood films. It follows recent events in the lives of a ladies' (and one man) small tap dancing class. And always remember, Ginger Rogers did everything Fred Astaire did but backwards *and* in high heels! The spectacular *Riverdance* reveals the historical mix of cultures.

British companies which show the roots of the jazz legacy are the Jiving Lindy-Hoppers, Zoots and Spangles, where performances include displays of the African influenced social dances of the 1940s and 50s like the *jitterbug* and the *jive*. Their style includes acrobatic partner work and jazzy steps in a typical relaxed, fluid style.

Disco dancing in its many forms has taken on a performance status of its own. It is a very competitive form with a large national network of events. People like Madonna and her association with the New York gay craze for *voguing* has influenced the style. In the past John Travolta and Michael Jackson have been the ones to follow. Other related styles imported across the Atlantic, along with their own designer fashions, are robotics, break-dancing, moon-walking and so on. They have all had their turn on the street, in the clubs and in competition. They have the street value of participation but the competitiveness often results in a shift of emphasis to performance and the more virtuosity the better!

A more homegrown version of showy club dancing is *bhangra*. Rooted in an ancient Punjabi celebration dance which is driven by a large loud drumbeat it has a fast and energetic style. Asian youth music and culture are pushing the boundaries on to blend ancient and modern movement, sounds and values. It is now not unusual to see the large Chinese communities of Britain performing their athletic lion or dragon dances in the streets to celebrate their new year. There is even a troupe of authentic Hawaiian hula dancers and a group of Appalachian clog dancers in Brighton, Sussex.

Of course we must not forget the ever-so-British ballroom dancing popularised by the BBC's *Come Dancing* programme. This is another style where participation was a priority, although nowadays the main aim seems to be to show competition and excellence in performance. In the 1920s famous dancers Vernon and Irene Castle danced the polite, refined foxtrot. This followed on from the waltz which had gripped Europe for a century in its hypnotic 3/4 rhythm. The technique of the ballroom's quickstep, foxtrot, waltzes and tangos became more and more rule-ridden, and this once social dancing of the upper classes declined in popularity and became a much more specialised cult pursuit. The 1920s brought a decline in musical standards of the big bands and fewer large ballrooms in favour of smaller, more intimate night clubs as fashions changed, reflecting the breakdown of the old British class structures. The West End glitter and glamour now subdued, the dancers moved out from London to the suburbs where there was space in the palais of the various large towns and cities.

The outbreak of World War II brought clothes rationing and the flowing fabrics so essential to the curving, fluid movements of dance had to be replaced with net (which was non-rationed). This gave a look of the – now familiar – ornately sequinned and jewelled yards of nylon net, which detracted from the original simple flow of the actual steps. Once again, a social dance transformed into competitive performance.

Finally in this section I would like to examine a style of performance so far not mentioned anywhere in the book. It is often included under the dance umbrella probably because of its non-verbal nature. It is *mime*. Such companies and artists as the Trestle Theatre Company and David Glass New Mime Ensemble and Peta Lily have done much to popularise an art which had a dusty old image. No longer the cliché of the thin man in his black tights and white gloves and face fighting his way through a strong wind or entrapped in an invisible box. Nowadays topics vary from Popeye to Shakespeare, Peter Pan to the Seven Samurai and much more.

SOCIAL DANCES

Many social dances have been mentioned in the previous section, but there are still more which keep their social label. The still popular folk-dance clubs are a nostalgic reminder of Britain's rich dance heritage, now largely lost. Some of the dances and songs were saved by the research of Cecil Sharp, founder of the English Folk Dance and Song Society.

In other parts of Europe ancient circle dances have been preserved and are still danced regularly as part of community celebrations. The steps are often simple and gently repetitive as they sweep everyone along into a higher plane of oneness with nature, each other and themselves. As such they hint at their pagan origins. They developed in pre-christian times to celebrate births, deaths, marriages and in Britain today circle dance is undergoing a revival. Many small groups are bringing a re-birth to old ways and values, not at odds with New Age politics, green awareness and concerns. Many are creating new music and steps as well as traditional ones, bringing the ancient into the here and now.

Scottish dancing has survived slightly better and, of all the forms, has retained a masculine identity for dance. In the face of many mis-representations dancing became wrongly associated with the effeminate. The performing of tippy-toe dancing from the 1800s through to the early 1900s classified dancers as either adored sylph or whimpish admirer. Only in the Scottish style did dancing on the toes remain a symbol of masculine strength, even in a skirt! The dance event at the Highland Games is just as masculine as tossing the caber. Of course the women dance too and there is a strong tradition of Scottish country dancing.

The other popular dance which reinforced male influence but actually banned women until recently was the *morris*. Its roots keep its social importance. The high leaps and athleticism are supposed to encourage the fertility and health of the community. Morris dancing would historically have been performed in the spring, at a time when the corn starts to grow; styles differ from one morris side to another and between different parts of the country. In the north it is a town dance, using very elaborate costume and clogs.

The pagan origins of morris give it its basic style. This has been influenced over the centuries by a number of social influences: the African *Moors* (*Moorish/morris*) came to Europe and it is said that this gave rise to the traditional blacking of the face, but others think that the sooted faces indicate something older than christianity. Many morris sides were lost in the time of the Industrial Revolution as isolated rural life declined. Other modifications to the morris over time have been a) the season: no longer linked to pagan festivals but performed at holiday times as dictated by industry and business; b) the costume: from whatever ribbons and bells etc could be afforded to elaborately designed everyday clothes, and c) nowadays morris sides arrive in their cars, not by foot! As in many male recreational activities, morris dancing is often an excuse for a few pints and perhaps a release from the stresses of the hectic pace of life in the twentieth century.

A few female sides exist even though there is still some disapproval. It is a strong tradition adapting and surviving with the times and continuing to give many the simple pleasure of joining in with dance.

In a different sphere which seems to be many worlds away from traditional British dancing is the long saga of clubs and discos, *rock 'n roll*, the *twist*, the *pogo* of punk, *reggae* and now the land of *house music* and *raves*. These temples of energetic endless dancing attract hundreds and thousands of people at a time. Most of it originated once again in the USA. The house music is relentless and often drug-assisted punters help maintain the tempo for hours. There is a massive financial profit to be made by the organisers but it is bringing back the simple pleasure of dance to many.

Another style of social dance which has achieved recent popularity in the 1990s is the Latin-American based *sambas*, *salsas* and *lambadas*, and the original type *tango*. Unlike raves these are dances for couples. There are many classes and social gatherings organised for these dances. In London there is even the London School of Samba where people can be in the samba band or the spectacular dance displays, reminiscent of Brazil's *Mardi Gras*. They also teach the dances to keen onlookers. Evenings end with everyone dancing together.

Britain in the twentieth century is a melting pot of different cultures and possibly one of the most exotic is Egyptian dance. Mostly performed by females, with its origins in the travelling entertainers in the first century BC, it is one of the most ancient dances known. In the Middle

East there is still a tradition of young men wearing braided hair and kohl on their eyes and dancing in the village streets. Its symbolic attachment to female fertility and healthy childbirth now inspires many British women. As a sophisticated dance technique its simple steps and graceful flow are enjoyed by many. This is a dance form which crosses the boundary as a form of fitness training too, which we will cover in the following section.

THE FITNESS FACTOR

'Working out' is now one of the most common kinds of exercise methods for women, but contrary to popular belief, it *did* exist pre-Fonda. Movement exercise to music has been popular since the 1930s and more recently 'aerobics' in various forms has boomed and is developing in many ways. This includes callanetics, step-classes, stretch n'tone, low-impact, high-impact and even competitions. As the exercises are performed the heart rate rises and so muscles are toned and the heart itself strengthened. Eventually there may be weight loss.

A wide variety of body conditioning activities with and without weights and/or machines are available and again can be taken to the dizzy heights of body building competitions. *Pilates* is one such method developed in the 1930s. It strengthens and conditions the body through a series of exercises performed in a balanced sequence. There is a good deal of attention to working isolated muscle groups through natural movements, often with machine assistance. It also encourages better posture.

The *Feldenkrais Method* is based on over 40 years research by Dr Moshe Feldenkrais. It uses gentle movement suitable for all ages and abilities and emphasises learning more intelligent ways of moving, so that stresses, aches and pains are reduced. This is typical of the type of fitness which works from an inner focus, unlike the more outward focuses of the Fonda world. Another such approach is the *Alexander Technique* which releases tension and teaches us how to use out bodies in a lighter, easier manner. This inner focus as a way of working owes much to the influence of Eastern philosophy. Yoga, tai'chi, shiatsu, massage and various healing techniques are available now more than ever. They are the New Age aerobics if you like!

Yoga is probably the best known and most popular technique. The word *yoga* means 'union' and it sets out to unify the mind, body and spirit in harmony with the universe. It exercises everything from internal organs to the hair on your head. Movement is slow with prolonged stillnesses emphasising breathing, stretching, relaxation, diet and positive thought through meditation. It is an ancient Hindu discipline dating back before it was written down in 300 BC.

Tai'chi and aikido both originate from the Far East and are gentle martial arts. They concentrate on meditation, relaxation, balance, flexibility and co-ordination. They are non-violent and aim to develop sensitive contact and control. Since the earliest classical period of Chinese medicine exercises to strengthen the constitution, enhance vitality and ensure good health have been a central part of the healing tradition. Influenced at different times by Taoist and Buddhist philosophies, by the theories of self-defence, the study of animal movement and natural science as much as by medical theories alone, these exercises belong to a rich traditional heritage. There are many different forms but all of them have in common a few central principles. These concern posture, breathing and mental concentration or visualisation and they are all concerned with promoting the subtle energy in the body which the Chinese call *chi*. The chi flows through a network of channels which connect internal organs with the rest of the body and help us to function harmoniously. Many forms of alternative medicine like acupuncture, reflexology and shiatsu are now easily available but not yet on the National Health shopping list.

Dance itself is used in therapy with elderly people or for those with learning difficulties. As such dance is non-elitist; it is for all. No longer is a multiple pirouette the only aim; moving a finger or a simple shake of a head can be dance and bring with it all the satisfaction of the grandest balletic movement. Often improvisation and contact improvisation are used. The decrease of stress, stimulating circulation and increasing muscle tone, even improving social skills are the aims of the work. There are obvious benefits to all types of people. We all need help to connect body and mind, or to release stress or simply to improve awareness of our self and others. In addition it is fun! The techniques used reflect eastern meditational body-mind theories. There are training courses in dance therapy.

So if we reflect on the fitness factor in Britain we see an interesting East-West divide. The hi-energy, body-beautiful politics that have reached our island from the United States contrasts with the gentler, more meditative approach of the East. This more holistic (*treat the person as a whole*), inside-out approach is often known as 'alternative'. You pays your money and you takes your choice!

DANCE TRAINING

At present you are probably studying dance for GCSE, A/S, A level or BTEC. You may be considering taking your dance education further and are wondering where you may be able to do so. There are lots of choices as the world of dance becomes more organised. No longer is the path one of local dancing school, then stage school or if you are lucky (and the correct height and weight) the Royal Ballet School. Neither is it true that you have to be young to train. Nowadays there are many different options other than performing. There is work in therapy, in notation, teaching, dance administration, research or in archives.

The chances to join in dance classes are many, whether in local studios, community centres or summer schools. These all build towards increasing levels of technical and choreographic skills, so that when applying for full-time training you have prepared yourself adequately. There are also many opportunities nationwide to join a youth dance group and if you look you will probably find one near you. These groups offer work in technique, choreography and performance.

Moving on to full-time training there are many fine colleges and schools in existence. Some are fee paying and subject to local authority discretionary awards. The Laban Centre, London Contemporary Dance School and the Rambert School are such places and are all of a very high standard, but the fees are high too. You may be fortunate to live in an enlightened authority who make discretionary grants available but these are few and far between. Most students will need a mandatory grant and their fees paid so the alternatives are the new universities which now offer dance-performance courses of a very high calibre and a degree at the end. MAs and PhDs are now more and more common too. There is also a range of courses for those who wish to go into teaching in schools or in the community. Posts of dance development officer are increasingly being created.

On most of the courses studies will include a range of dance techniques; composition; dance criticism and aesthetics; history; notation; anatomy and physiology; teaching methods; music; stage design; arts administration.

Other avenues of training are in the aerobics and fitness areas. Often these involve working on short courses, or in the more holistic styles it can involve close association with an expert in that particular field. In all these types of training you would have to be self-financing.

So you can see in the world of dance nowadays there are many choices. There is still the traditional route into performing with a ballet company or in West End shows, pop videos, nightclubs and television.

In the appendix there is a list of useful addresses. It is by no means comprehensive but will help you to make a start in finding a course to suit you. Who knows what will happen next? There are always surprises in store. It may even be *you* who, through your study and training, discovers dance in yet another new way. At the very least it is well worth thinking about dance as being a rich part of your life – whether as dancer, choreographer, administrator or audience. Perhaps you feel that you are not destined to be a dancer but a dancing computer operator, shop assistant, engineer or politician. For those of you who are going into training for other careers, try to keep your dancing alive as a refreshing part of your life. The world needs dancing accountants, scientists and politicians!

Dance is for life – so live it!

REFERENCES

Further Reading

Magazines

Dance and Dancers (monthly), Plusloop Ltd, 248 High St, Croydon, CR0 1NF. Tel. 0181 681 7817

Dance Theatre Journal (quarterly), Laban Centre, Laurie Grove, London SE14 6NH. Tel. 0181 692 4070

Dancing Times (monthly), Clerkenwell House, 45-7 Clerkenwell Green, London EC1R 0BE.

Book/video sources

Dance Books, 9 Cecil Court, London WC2N 4EZ. Tel. 0171 836 2314

National Resource Centre For Dance, University of Surrey, Guildford, GU2 5XH. Tel. 01483 509316

The Data Place/The Video Place, 17 Duke's Rd, London WC1H 9AB. Tel. 0171 387 0161

Course/Activity Information Sources

Dance Directory (1991) ed T. Connolly, Mentor.

Survey of Courses Leading to the BTEC National Diploma in the Performing Arts, HMSO, 1990.

On The Move, directory of dance and movement activities for young people, from the Community Dance and Mime Foundation, School of Arts, De Montfort University, Scraptoft Campus, Leicester LE7 9SU. Tel. 01533 418517.

The Council For Dance, Education and Training, 5 Tavistock Place, London, WC1H 9SS. Tel. 0171 388 5770.

Books

The Encyclopedia of Dance and Ballet (1977) eds. Mary Clarke and David Vaughan, Pitman Publishing.

Let's Dance (1978) P. Buckingham, Paddington Press, London. (History of ballroom, social and folk dance.)

GLOSSARY

Abstraction. A process of reducing something to its most basic form.

Accent. Stress on a beat or movement.

Actions. The five dance skills of travel, turn, jump, stillness and gesture.

Aerobic. Exercise which develops cardiovascular (of the heart) endurance and uses oxygen.

Alignment. Proper posture as near to a straight line as possible from head to toe when standing.

Asymmetry. Uneven in space, time or dynamics.

Ballet. A highly stylised technique of dance started in Europe in the 15th century.

Beat. The underlying pulse of regular movement or music.

Bounce. A small springy movement.

Canon. An overlap in the dancers' movements.

Centering. Bringing together the physical centre with that of the mind.

Choreography. The art of arranging movement into a meaningful whole.

Climax. The main highpoint of a dance.

Communication. The projection by the dancer to the audience of the content of the dance.

Complementary. Movements which are similar but not the same.

Contemporary dance. see **Modern dance.**

Content. The central idea of the dance.

Contact improvisation. Spontaneous movement to support, bounce off and onto etc a partner or group.

Contraction. Muscular shortening that changes the shape of a limb. In Graham technique contraction of the torso is a main principle.

Contrast. Movements unlike those in the main theme of a dance.

Counts. The number of beats within the measure.

Criticism. A judgement of a dance based on careful consideration of choreographic and technical principles.

Design. Planning movement in time and space.

Development. Altering the action, space, time and quality of motifs so that when they are repeated they remain interesting.

Direction. Movement possibilities to front, back, side and the four diagonals.

Downstage. The space towards the front of the stage.

Dynamics. The variety of force, accent and quality of movement.

Effort actions. When weight, time and space are combined, eight possible ways of moving result. As identified by Rudolf Laban.

Elevation. Jumping or rising.

Enchainment. A linked series of movement.

Energy. Potential to move.

Extension. The lengthening of body parts an important factor in a dancer's training.

Fall. A controlled movement towards the floor either a total collapse or followed by a recovery.

Flexibility. The range of movement possible in the joints. It is important to increase this in dance training.

Flexion. Movement when a joint bends.

Flow. a. free or bound in movement.

b. flexible or direct through space.

c. successive or simultaneous through the body.

(As named by Rudolf Laban.)

Focus. The dancer's sight line used to increase communication with the audience.

Force. Intensity of weight, ranging from firm to light.

Form. The structure of a planned dance composition which organises the themes and motifs.

Frontal plane. Gives rise to elevation.

Fugue. (in music and dance). The theme is varied and played versus itself.

Gesture. Movements which do not transfer or bear weight.

Group movement. To dance in relation to others by taking cues from each other.

Ground bass. A structure in which the basic theme is repeated in the background or other thematic movement.

Highlights. The movements of greater visual note in a dance.

Horizontal plane. Gives rise to opening and closing/turning.

Improvisation. Unplanned exploration in movement.

Isolation. Movement restricted to a single joint or muscle group, frequently used in Jazz Dance.

Jazz dance. A style of dance originally from the African slaves in the south of the United States of America. Now often used in shows and musicals.

Jeté. A leap.

Joints. A place where two bones meet. There are four types which allow for varying amounts of movement.

Kinaesthetic. Sensing through nerves to muscles of body positions, movement and tension.

Leap. Elevation. Take off on one foot and land on the other.

Level. An aspect of space ranging from high to low through medium.

Ligament. A band of tough tissue which connects bones.

Locomotor. Movement which crosses the space.

Mark. Rehearsing movement without going flat-out.

Measures. Groups of beats separated by bars into intervals.

Metre. Notes how many beats are in a measure.

Modern dance. A dance genre which emphasizes the importance of choreographers' choice of theme, intent and style.

Motif. The central movement theme of a dance which is repeated, developed and varied.

Muscle. Groups of fibres which contract and extend to produce movement.

Nervous system. The brain, spinal cord and nerves that send messages to the muscles to produce movement.

New dance. A style of dance in Britain which has evolved as a reaction against more traditional contemporary styles.

Opposition. A natural movement of an opposite body part to maintain balance.

Pace. The overall speed of sections of a dance.

Parallel. When standing the thighs, knees and toes facing directly forwards.

Percussive. A quality of movement which has sharp starts and stops.

Phrase. A sentence of movement of varying lengths.

Placement. Balanced alignment of level hips; legs placed in line with the hips, shoulders relaxed, spine extended, abdominal area lifted.

Plane. The result of joining two dimensions.

Plié. A bend of the knees keeping the body aligned.

Positions. The five positions of the feet in ballet, as invented in 17th century France.

Post modern dance. Started in New York in the 1960s to experiment with what dance could be.

Proscenium. The frame of the stage through which dance is seen.

Quality. This is determined by the varied use of weight and dynamics eg percussive, swings, vibrate.

Release. Letting go of tension. In Graham technique it usually follows a contraction. In new dance it is used to relax the body and mind so as to encourage ease of movement and creativity.

Relevé. Raised on half-toe.

Rhythm. A structure of movement patterns in time.

Rotation. Movement that turns around the long axis of a bone.

Sagittal. A plane which gives rise to advancing/retreating movements.

Shape. Design of body parts of one or more dancers.

Size. From small to large. An aspect of space that may be used to vary motifs.

Skeleton. The frame of bones that supports the body.

Sonata. A structure in music which uses three or four contrasting rhythms and moods that relate in tone and style.

Spotting. During turning the eyes fix on a spot and the head is quickly brought round at the last possible moment to refocus on the spot again. Avoids dizziness.

Stimulus. A starting point which triggers ideas for movement.

Strength. Muscle power to be increased through dance training.

Stretch. Range of movement in a joint to be increased by lengthening muscles through dance training.

Style. An individual manner of choreography or performing.

Suspension. A floating, effortless light quality of movement.

Sustained. A constant, continuous smooth movement.

Swing. Pendulum-like movement with an easy natural feel.

Symmetry. Balanced or even in time, space or dynamics.

Syncopation. Stress on the beat which is not in the usual place.

Technique. Skill in dance movement.

Tempo. The speed of the movement or music.

Tendon. Tough chords which end muscles and connect them to the bones.

Transition. Links between movement themes, motifs, phrases or sections.

Triplets. A three step pattern.

Turn-out. The outward rotation of the legs from the hips.

Unison. Dancers moving at the same time.

Unity. A sense of an harmonious whole in the dance form.

Upstage. The space towards the back of the stage.

Variation. A motif or theme is modified without losing its character.

Vertebrae. Single bones that make up the spine.

Vibratory. A quality of movement which is jittery—fast stops and starts.

Warm up. Muscle preparation for exercise to avoid injury.

Xylophone. A musical instrument of flat heavy wooden bars struck with a hammer.

Yoga. Hindu system of relaxation and mediation.

Zapateado. A dance with rhythmic stamping of the feet.

USEFUL ADDRESSES

A. TRAINING TO DANCE IN BRITAIN

Bedford College of Higher Education, 37 Lansdowne Rd, Bedford MK40 2BZ. Tel. 01234 351966

Bretton Hall College of Higher Education, West Bretton, Wakefield, West Yorkshire WF4 4LG. Tel. 01924 830261

University of Brighton, Chelsea School of Human Movement, Trevin Towers, Gaudick Rd, Eastbourne BN20 7SP. Tel. 01273 600900

University of Central England in Birmingham, Westbourne Rd, Edgbaston, Birmingham. Tel. 0121 4545106

Crewe + Alsager Faculty, The Manchester Metropolitan University, Alsager ST7 2HL. Tel. 0193 633231

De Montfort University, Scraptoft Campus, Leicester LE7 9SU. Tel. 01533 431011

Laban Centre for Dance, Laurie Grove, New Cross, London SE14 6NH. Tel. 0181 692 4070

London Contemporary Dance School, The Place, 17 Dukes Rd, WC1H 9AB. Tel. 0171 387 0324

Liverpool John Moores University, Barkhill Rd, Liverpool L17 6BD. Tel. 0151 724 2321

London College of Dance, (ISTD), 10 Linden Rd, Bedford, MK40 2DA. Tel. 01234 213331

Middlesex University, Trent Park, Cockfosters Rd, Barnet, Herts EN4 0PT. Tel. 0181 440 5181

Rambert Dance School, 94 Chiswick High Rd, London W4 1SH. Tel. 0181 995 4246

Roehampton Institute, Roehampton Lane, London SW15 5PJ. Tel. 0181 878 5751

College of Royal Academy of Dancing, 48 Vicarage Crescent, London SW11 3LT. Tel. 0181 223 0091

University of Surrey, Guildford GU2 5XH. Tel. 01483 571281

West Sussex Institute of Higher Education, Bishop Otter College, College Lane, Chichester, West Sussex PO19 4PE. Tel. 01243 787911

Please note that this is not an exhaustive list and there are other centres. It is also worth checking to see if your local technical college offers any A-level, BTEC or HNC dance courses.

OTHER ADDRESSES

Dance Books, 9 Cecil Court, London WC2N 4EZ

Dance Umbrella, Riverside Studios, Crisp Rd, London. Tel. 0171 741 4040

Dance Theatre Journal, (quarterly), Laban Centre, Laurie Grove, London SE14 6NH

British Ballet Organisation, Woolborough House, 39 Lonsdale Rd, London SW13 9PJ

INDEX